The Dark Side of the Inner Child

"AWAKENING" is a key word: It means we have awakened from our personal vantage point or perspective. Everything looks totally different...to be freed from that vantage point and awaken from that vantage point so that you suddenly see everything differently—and the practical application of this awakening...is that you change.

Pir Vilayat Inayat Khan

The paper used in this publication meets the minimum requirements of American National Standard for Information Sciences— Permanence of Paper for Printed Library Materials, ANSI Z39.48-1984.

The Dark Side of the Inner Child

The Next Step

Stephen Wolinsky

BRAMBLE ❖ BOOKS

Connecticut

For information write to:
Bramble Books, PO Box 209, Norfolk, Connecticut 06058

Library of Congress Cataloging-in-Publication Data

Wolinsky, Stephen
    The dark side of the inner child : the next step / Stephen Wolinsky.
        p.   cm.
    Includes bibliographical references and index.
    ISBN 1-883647-00-2 (pbk.) : $14.95
    1. Inner child. 2. Schemas (Pscyhology) 3. Schema-focused cognitive therapy. 4. Cognitive dissonance. I. Title.
    BF698.35.I55W65 1993
    155.2'5—dc20   93-41991
                                                      CIP

First Printing 1993
1 3 5 7 9 10 8 6 4 2

Printed in the United States of America

DEDICATION

To the memory of John Lennon, Quantum Psychologies Poet and Song-writer.

ACKNOWLEDGMENTS

Kristi L. Kennen, M.S.W., Lynne Behnfield (copy editor), Donna Ross and Bruce Carter (word processing), Eric Marcus, M.D., Roberto Assagioli, founder of Psychosynthesis and developer of the concept of subpersonalities, Fritz Perls, M.D., founder of Gestalt Therapy, for his idea of parts dialoguing with each other, and Eric Berne, M.D., founder of Transactional Analysis and creator of the understanding of the inner parent, inner adult, and inner child. Also thanks to Dr. Albert Ellis, the father of Rational-Emotive Thearpy, whose understanding of the fifteen distorted thinking types were incorporated in this book, and to Mathew McKay, Martha Davis, and Patrick Fanning for their book, *Thoughts and Feelings: The Art of Cognitive Stress Intervention.* Chapter 3 of this book contains a summary of Dr. Albert Ellis's fifteen cognitive distortions. Finally, special thanks to Neil Sweeny, and his memory for his consultation, love, and friendship for almost 20 years.

The Author

Stephen H. Wolinsky, Ph.D., began his clinical practice in Los Angeles, California in 1974. A Gestalt and Reichian therapist and trainer, he led workshops in Southern California. He was also trained in Classical Hypnosis, Psychosynthesis, Psychodrama/Psychomotor, and Transactional Analysis. In 1977 he journeyed to India, where he lived for almost six years studying meditation. He moved to New Mexico in 1982 to resume a clinical practice. There he began to train therapists in Ericksonian Hypnosis, N.L.P. and family therapy. Dr. Wolinsky also conducted year-long trainings entitled: Integrating Hypnosis with Psychotherapy, and Integrating Hypnosis with Family Therapy. Dr. Wolinsky is the author of *Trances People Live: Healing Approaches in Quantum Psychology*®, and *Quantum Consciousness: The Guide to Experiencing Quantum Psychology*® (Bramble Books). He has just completed his fourth book, *The Tao of Chaos: Essence and the Enneagram, Quantum Consciousness, Volume II*. He is the co-developer of Quantum Seminars™ and the founder of Quantum Psychology®. Along with Kristi L. Kennen, M.S.W., he founded the first Quantum Psychology Institute®. For more information about workshops and seminars write: Quantum Psychology Institute®, c/o The Bramble Company, PO Box 209, Norfolk, CT 06058, or call Dr. Stephen Wolinsky at 0 (700) 661-1993.

Table of Contents

Foreword

I welcome the opportunity to write this forward for Dr. Stephen Wolinsky's *The Dark Side of the Inner Child*. This book further attests to the seriousness of inner child work. It offers some important clarifications with regard to the tendency to "reify" certain aspects of inner child work. Dr. Wolinsky has helped me understand my own work more precisely.

For a number of years I've been impressed with the transforming "power" of the inner child model. Yet I never fully understood why it makes such an impact. Wolinsky's earlier work *Trances People Live*, which identifies certain childhood survival tactics as hypnotic trances, made it clear to me that the reason we stay frozen in the past is because we keep recreating the trances which defend us from the hurt and pain of our childhood losses. The "delayed grief" apropos of these losses manifests itself in a set of symptoms which have been called the "adult child syndrome".

Dr. Wolinsky shows clearly that since we created the defending trances, we can change them once we are aware of how we're continuing to create them. What I have called *reclaiming* the inner child is a way to dehypnotize oneself. By imagining ourselves embracing our vulnerability in the form of a little child, our adult self takes charge of a trance that originally protected us, but now limits us. What I called championing the child is a way to live in the present moment, by consciously changing the ways we have been rejecting our own childhood feelings, needs, and wants.

In *The Dark Side of the Inner Child*, Wolinsky offers us a

variety of ways to become aware of how we are creating the defensive trances that constitute the frozen states of the inner child.

I have stressed the essential role of one's adult self in reintegrating the experiences of the past. Wolinsky speaks of the "witnessing self." The adult in my model and the witnessing self are *roughly* equivalent. The adult of witnessing self is the one who created the trances in the first place. The witnessing self is the I of I or the you of you.

When we grasp that we are the true source of our own frozen life, an empowering enlightenment takes place and adult responsibility follows.

Wolinsky's work thus serves the important task of safeguarding the regressive tendencies inherent in inner child work. For whether we intend to are not, there is an ever present temptation to "objectify" the inner child so that the various states of childhood being are given a kind of functional autonomy. Once this happens, the "inner child" is idealized and becomes an end in itself. With Wolinsky's work, there can be no confusion on this point.

The inner child is *not all precious and wonderful*. By grasping the ways we continue to use the frozen and outdated trances of survival, we deprive ourselves of some essential areas of human experience. These areas include behaviors like curiosity, questioning, resiliency, exuberance, and spontaneity. Wolinsky calls this limiting function the *"dark side of the inner child"*. We need our feelings of curiosity, spontaneity, and exuberance. We need the ability to question and be resilient. These are not just childhood traits, they are human traits, essential to fully functioning human beings. By *consciously* choosing to *reform* our childhood strategies for survival (the trances of the inner child), we can gain access to emotions which comprise our "delayed grief" and fully experience them. This allows us to integrate these crucial functions into our experiences, making us more fully present to live our *own* lives.

I don't want to expound on the text any further because I hope you will want to read it yourself. I have found a very rich and creative body of material in the chapters which follow. You may find it tough going at times, and I urge you to hang in there. The mental stretch has been well worth the effort for me.

I want to thank Dr. Wolinsky for his commitment to expand our consciousness. He brings together a syntheses of the most profound

Eastern and Western thinking. In an age that is ravished by self-serving polarizations, Wolinsky is a most welcome teacher.

John Bradshaw

•Prologue

Woman, I know you understand ...the little child inside of the man.

"Woman" John Lennon

In 1985 I made a discovery that culminated in my first book, *Trances People Live: Healing Approaches in Quantum Psychology.* In it I describe the trance phenomenon involved in problem states. I show how trance is the means by which symptoms are created and maintained and become a source of pathology as they are integrated in our habitual mode of response to the world. Most important, I explain how we can de-hypnotize ourselves and re-claim the true self.

The response to the book has been sensational, yet I feel a more experiential, practical, and user-friendly version is needed. That book was directed to the therapist; this is for the general public as well as the therapeutic community.

About the Inner Child

As I wrote in my earliest book, the trance process can often times be traced back to childhood experiences of trauma. The observer creates trance states in childhood and uses them to help in *buffering* the child against the experiences they are not able to

1

integrate. In other words, trances often start as a necessary means of surviving and negotiating the physical universe.

Yet what was a survival strategy for an overwhelmed child attempting to cope with chaos becomes the core of symptom structure for the coping adult. Not to be confused with the so-called *precious inner child* now so popular in therapeutic circles, this is a wounded inner child stuck at a particular point in time.

The words *inner child* have drawn much fire from different schools of psychotherapy. Actually, to clarify, the inner child concept is not new. In the Psychosynthesis of Roberto Assagioli, he talks of *subpersonalities*. In the Gestalt Therapy of Fritz Perls, he developed the experience of having different *parts* dialoguing with one another, the work of Eric Berne, M.D., called Transactional Analysis, developed not only the inner child, but the inner adult, and the inner parent. In discussing the cognitive therapy of Dr. Albert Ellis, Aaron Beck, M.D. talks of a similar concept called *Schemas*.

A second major concept in the cognitive model consists of the concept of *Schemas*. The concept is used to explain why a depressed patient maintains his pain-inducing and self-defeating attitudes despite objective evidence of positive factors in his life.

Any situation is composed of a plethora of stimuli. An individual selectively attends to specific stimuli, combines them in a pattern and conceptualizes the situation. Although different persons may conceptualize the same situation in different ways, a particular person tends to be consistent in his response to similar types or events. Relatively stable cognitive patterns form the basis for the regularity of interpretations of a particular set of situations. The term *Schema* designates these stable cognitive patterns.

When a person faces a particular circumstance, the *Schema* related to the circumstance is *activated*. The *Schema* is the basis for molding data into cognitions (defined as any ideation with verbal or pictorial content). Thus a *Schema* constitutes the basis for screening out, differentiating, and coding stimuli that confront the individual. He categorizes and evaluates his experiences through a matrix of *Schemas*.

The kinds of *Schemas* employed determine how an individual will structure different experiences. A *Schema* may be inactive for long periods of time but can be energized by specific environmental inputs (for example, stressful situations). The schemas activated in a specific situation directly determine how an individual responds. (Beck, 1979:12-13)

The world view of the child is time frozen, unbeknownst to the adult (this is a *Schema*). The adult in present time is, in effect, *hypnotized* by the wounded inner child's schema and reacts automatically, so that life is not experienced as it *is* in the present moment, but rather as it *was* in the past. It is the resistance to an event that keeps the memory of the event stuck in ones consciousness. The father of Cognitive Therapy, Dr. Albert Ellis says, "the child tells itself that certain bad events *must not* occur...which keeps recreating them...to use your terminology, the child traumatizes itself..." (Albert Ellis, a personal letter). Therefore, whether we call it the inner child schema, inner child subpersonality, the inner child parts, or the inner child false self, we are talking about a time-frozen position which acts as a way the child within views experiences and interprets the outer world.

The Inner Child

In reality, just as there are numerous *subpersonalities, false selves* or *schemas* that are constructed, we can also say there is not just one inner child. Rather there are numerous *inner children*, each with a different perception, a different awareness, a different world view, etc. (See Illustration #1, page 4).

This is, therefore, an inner child with a *dark side*; rather than being just *precious*, it has a dysfunctional shadow side. One of the purposes of this book is to get the reader in touch with that frozen, inner-child memory that keeps creating problems by filtering reality through outmoded, limited, and distorted lenses.

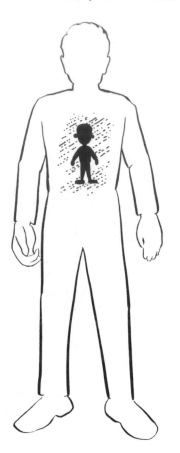 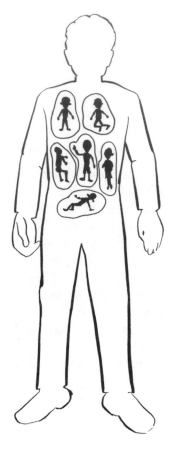

Not one inner child or Schema   **Many inner children or Schema**

Illustration #1

This illustration shows a picture of not one, but many inner children.

Conventional professional therapy would try to change the inner child's view, to re-frame it, "complete" its unfinished business, or "champion" it. In psychotherapy, a client might present a frozen memory-like picture in his or her mind of a parent doing something abusive to him/her. The therapist might then ask the client to "miniaturize" him/herself and "go into" the picture to re-experience the trauma and all its attendant pain and suffering. Many therapies would at that point introduce a new belief, for example, "It's okay to trust men," or, "People do love me."

The intention of these therapies is to "heal the inner child." *What I propose is dramatically different.*

Quantum Psychology

The first tenet of Quantum Psychology is that *subjective, internal* reality is *observer*-created. You, as the observer of a trauma, take a picture of it, hold it, merge with it, go to sleep, and then go on the same tape-loop ride over and over again. Quantum Psychology says that *you, (the observer),* hold and create the inner-child memory in response to a trauma. To clarify, the observer does not create the outer event. The observer creates it's *response* to the outer event. Therefore, the observer, who has fallen asleep and fused with the memory, must be *awakened* so that the memory can be let go of by the observer.

That *picture* that is given the power is a memory that you *(the observer)* are holding. It's an old movie that you re-run again and again causing the old feelings and experiences to be felt over and over. In my work, rather than empowering an inner child or memory, we *empower you,* the one who *observes* and holds the memory in place. According to Albert Ellis, "It is your *must* that the memory *must not have existed* that is given the real power, not the picture itself" (Ellis, personal letter). Here, I would say it is the *observer* who holds the memory in place by resisting the memory. Ellis thinks, however, that the primary glue that holds the memory in place is the *must not have occurred* thought.

In the process presented here, you learn to identify what the inner child is doing so hte *observer* can awaken and stop identifying with those old trances. This enables you to begin to identify with the *observer* you that is free of trances. This frees you from the wounded inner child that is stuck, so you can live fully in present time.

This book is about going beyond the trances, outdated strategies and belief structures created in childhood to cope with the *chaos* of life. The text is full of examples and exercises to help you identify and free yourself from the trances operating in your life that are preventing you from being who you really are. The exercises are also designed to help professionals work with their clients in accomplishing these same goals.

Although this is not the total focus of the book, it is important to state again that there is not just one wounded inner child. Rather, with each perceived trauma, the *observer* creates a strategy (trance) and an identity to manage the perceived chaos. Hence, within the adult there can be numerous inner children, each with a trance, a strategy, and an identity. This accounts for the numerous internal arguments that occur within an adult. They are the wounded inner children, each with an identity, each with a trauma and memory, each with a trance strategy, and each with an agenda. This explains why in therapy the entire resolution of problems does not occur once the inner child is located and "labeled." A new inner child pops up, hypnotizing the adult into another problem state using a *must not have occurred* thought.

This book is about going beyond the dark side of the inner child, and the trances of the inner child. To awaken the *observer/creator* of the inner child is to end the trances of the inner child. In other words, awakening the *observer* ends the trance. Stated another way, to transcend the frozen states of the inner child you must end your trances. This is the real process of *trance*-ending.. I hope you enjoy the process.

With love,
Your brother,
Stephen

•1

Where it All
Began for Me

For almost six years, I lived in a monastery in India. Before that, I conducted a private psychotherapy and training practice in Los Angeles, California. While in India it became apparent to me that meditation could be seen as an Eastern way of de-hypnotizing myself from my mental program, i.e., thoughts, feelings, and emotions.

By de-hypnotizing myself I no longer felt compelled nor obsessed by the never ending chatter of the mind.

A New Understanding of
Trances and Hypnosis

Some people feel that trance and hypnosis are similar to the *Svengali Phenomenon*, in which the subject is overpowered and instructed to do something against his/her will, by an outside *power* or person. Sometimes hypnosis is thought of as a state resembling sleep, induced by a hypnotizer, who makes suggestions readily accepted by the subject. "Trance" is defined by *Webster's* as

"a state of partly suspended animation or inability to function, a state of prolonged absorption." (American College Dictionary, Random House, New York, 1963:1285)

From my years of psycho-spiritual inner work, it became clear to me that we are all already in a trance, already hypnotized. Most of us think "trances" exclude our daily experience, but actually they engulf our every experience. Within the mystery of hypnosis or trance lies the key to de-hypnosis.

What will follow are examples and histories of everyday people being "entranced."

A child is the subject, the mom and dad the hypnotists. The parents make suggestions like "You're not going to make it," "Please me and I'll please you," or "Do what I say and I'll give you love and approval; don't and I won't." The child (subject) goes into a trance, a state of absorption, and believes the suggestions that the hypnotists (parents) make. The child then internalizes these suggestions and continues to suggest them as a grown adult. This is the *dark side of the inner child*, the inner child of the past hypnotizing the present time adult into problem states.

As years go on, perhaps a teacher or another authority figure merely mentions the similar suggestion (induction), and the subject (student) goes into the same "fear" trance that happened as a child. Time goes on. The child matures, enters into relationships, and marries. Then the spouse can become the hypnotist, putting the inner child of their spouse in an anger trance or a fear of rejection trance.

Once the suggestions are made and the individual moves into a trance, the subject's autonomy as a free being behind these trance states is lost.

In our culture we all go in and out of trance states, and each of us acts as both hypnotist and subject, through most of our relationships.

The purpose of this book is to *awaken the you* behind the trance, so that problems that are caused by trance states no longer can occur.

Self-hypnosis and trance *happen daily*. If you notice the movement of the mind, you are continually offering suggestions to yourself about how to be, what to do, and what to have.

For example, you might suggest to yourself in your relationship, "He really loves me," creating a relaxed "He really loves me" trance. You might suggest to yourself, "She never gives me what I want," creating an angry trance. You might suggest to yourself, "I know what that (boss) wants; he wants to "cheat me," creating a self-righteous trance.

All of these tapes are played by the inner child within the adult. The child within takes on the voices and suggestions of parents, and years later the child within the adult hypnotizes the adult.

How does this occur? Generally, we create trances as children to handle situations that we think we cannot handle nor understand. Albert Ellis would say, "We create profound musturbatory beliefs about many instances." (Ellis, personal letter) The ones we decide we must not, should not or can not handle. These *musts* act as cognitive glue which hold our resistance to incoming situations or circumstances. This *must not* thinking tendency greatly influences our subjective experience, and Dr. Albert Ellis calls this tendency, jokingly, musturbation.

For example, A child of an overbearing parent will disconnect from the situation to avoid the emotional pain. If the strategy works, the child puts the trance on "automatic." He finds himself disconnecting and daydreaming through school, work, and eventually in relationships.

A child who has a history of alcoholism and co-dependence in the family might exhibit **amnesia,** forget the past to avoid the pain. Later in life amnesia or forgetfulness might become a problem in work, school, or relationships.

An incest survivor who went "numb" to survive the painful trauma may experience difficulty feeling sensations during sexual experiences. Women may have an inability to have an orgasm. Men could suffer from premature ejaculation or impotency.

It must be understood that the trance a child created is actually an ability or skill that was developed to handle painful situations. The problem occurs when the ability to create a trance gets out of control, and the individual **finds himself** reacting automatically. The trance of the child within the adult automatically creates the same state of numbness even though the adult might not want to be numb in the present-time relationship. All this occurs while the *observer* sleeps.

For example, a woman I worked with was so badly spanked by her father that from the waist down she was numb. This affected her sexual relationship with her husband. She could not feel "sexual" sensations, and had an inability to achieve orgasm.

A psychologist I saw for therapy is another example. He had had an incestuous relationship with his sister. Years later in his marriage, the child within his adult world "went numb." The presenting problem: the ability to have an erection.

If you experience yourself reacting emotionally or verbally on "automatic," you might be experiencing an hypnotic trance suggested by the child within the adult. The child within hypnotizes the child by **automatically** saying things to you that make you go into a trance. You behave in ways you would rather not, or you may go into a trance that worked under trauma in the past, but is not appropriate for the present-time situation.

The child within becomes your hypnotist, and *the adult* in present time, the subject, continues getting hypnotized into unwanted behaviors and experiences.

After returning to the West in 1982, I re-opened my psychotherapy practice. I began to explore with my clients and trainees therapeutic trance states. I realized that many problems individuals were experiencing were due to the child within hypnotizing the adult. The inner child had developed an autonomous life of its own, a *dark side*.

I began to de-hypnotize myself. I realized that hours of meditation was not appropriate for this culture; it is just too time consuming. The pitfalls meditators experienced in the past resulted from not being connected to the world. And often times, as will be noted in Chapter 6, Dis-connecting, meditation can become a dissociative technique, used to hide a trauma and its accompanying fear, pain, and anger.

I was interested in developing a system that incorporates both (a) the ability to de-hypnotize oneself while (b) staying connected to life. To do this I incorporated a major concept of quantum physics: the observer of an internal experience is also *participating* in the internal subjective creation of that experience. In my earlier work, *Quantum Consciousness*, this was explored in depth. In essence, the observer of a trauma creates his/her *response* to the trauma. This often creates a wounded, traumatized child who uses trance states like "going numb" to survive.

The child within me had erected strategies to handle life situations. The problem was that the child within my adult self was creating internal experiences outside my awareness that did not fit my present-time reality.

A system of self-awareness began to evolve for me. I began to feel free of unwanted behaviors and emotions that had been suggested by the child within the adult.

Later chapters take an in-depth look at the trances of the inner child, the time frozen creation and identity within the adult. This inner child, which has received so much praise for so long, is a time frozen creation of the observer, you. The problem is that the time frozen inner child keeps creating *unwanted* trances, i.e., thoughts, feelings, emotions, sensations and strategies that no longer fit present-time situations.

Conclusion

The next step is to dismantle time-frozen, inner-child trances and realize that the individual is the *observer* and creator of this time-frozen inner-child identity. The purpose is to free ourselves from childhood survival mechanisms that no longer fit present-time relationships. The *next step* has three parts, 1) to acknowledge the *dark side* of the inner child which acts as a hypnotist in our present time self, 2) to look at this inner child identity, and release it from our present time reality, and 3) to awaken the *observer* (you), who has fallen asleep. This enables us to step out of our time-frozen past and step into being present in present time.

•2

The Beginning of the End of the Dark Side of the Inner Child

The recent emergence and popularity of therapies and self-help groups based on working on or with the "wounded inner child" has taken over the world of psychology. Historically speaking, however, most therapies have spoken directly to this part of ourselves that remains in past time, or was frozen in past time through trauma or mishap since psychotherapy became popular at the turn of the century.

More recently, since the 1960s, our psyches have been bombarded by therapies whose intention is to heal, re-frame, re-decision, talk to, re-associate, re-name, complete the unfinished business of, and most recently to champion the wounded inner child.

This precious inner child, as he/she has most recently been called is some wounded part of ourselves that needs to be healed. Somehow, and for some reason, two aspects of this paradigm have been left out. First, the source of the wounded inner child, and second, the dark side of the inner child.

Where did the Inner Child Come From?

To best understand where the inner child came from it is probably important to touch one of the most significant understandings of science. In the mid-1920s, noted physicist Werner Heisenberg developed his *"Uncertainty Principle."* Heisenberg, turned the world of physics around when he proved that the *observer* of the experiment and the experiment were not separate—but in fact, the *observer* through the act of observation participated and influenced the outcome of the experiment. John Wheeler, another noted physicist changed the word *observer* to *participator*, because the act of *observation participated* in the outcome of the experiment.

What does this mean in self-help psychology talk? That you, as the observer of life, participate in how you construct, interpret and experience your internal subjective world. The *observer* of an experiment participates in the creation of it's outcome through the act of observation. *You*, as the participator in a workshop on the inner child, create its appearance through the act of *observation*. What does this mean? By looking for the inner child, you recreate it through the act of "looking." It appears that the wounded inner child was always there, unnoticed. But, according to quantum physics, we create an inner child identity that needs to be healed through the act of "looking." The important thing to note at this stage of the book is that you (the *observer*) came before and are *senior* to the inner child identity. What I mean by this is that the *observer* existed *before* a trauma, the same observer was there *during* the trauma, and the same *observer* is there *after* the trauma ended. The inner child *I*-dentity is the cause of many of your present-time problems. Why? The wounded inner child you have *participated* in creating has a life-force of it's own, and limits your scope and perspective of the world and yourself. Furthermore, this *observer-created* identity creates behavioral inevitabilities like failure, break-up, or emotional distress. What we will focus on are the strategies, trances, or games, the dark side of the inner child plays, that effect your life. And, how to take the *next step* and awaken the *observer* and dismantle this past memory that acts as a window we look through in present time.

In the 1970s and 1980s, all of us saw the unparalleled everyday use of the word "quantum." From television shows to chemical corporations, *quantum* became a household world.

In 1986, my first book, *Trances People Live: Healing Approaches in Quantum Psychology*, talked of the impact of the *observer* (you) upon your subjective experience. In a nutshell, the *observer* (you), creates his/her *internal subjective experience*. You create a response to the environment, i.e., parents, teachers, husbands, wives, etc., and you are responsible for your internal, subjective experiences. To put this in Quantum Psychology terms, you, as the *observer* of external reality, *participate in the creation of your internal, subjective responses and reactions.*

Now, let's take this in the realm of the "wounded inner child identity." Let's say at a young age, you observed that the only way to get loved by Mom/Dad was to give up your own needs in favor of theirs and to please them. To handle this the *observer creates* an identity called "pleasing child" who gives up his/her own needs to gain love and approval. If the *observer* sees that this works, the *observer* continues to create this identity and places this identity of wounded pleasing child on automatic and then goes to sleep. Who is lost in this mistaken identity? You, the *observer* and creator of this pleasing wounded child identity.

This identity now creates many different ways (which will be discussed later) to keep this process alive. Three important points come from this quantum understanding: (1) you are the creator and *observer* of the wounded pleasing child, (2) you are beyond this identity, and (3) "healing" this wounded child is a false concept. Why? In order to heal this identity you must "get" that you are the *source* of this identity. Once you get the experiential understanding of this, you can take *responsibility for creating it and stop creating it.*

To try to heal, say the "right things" to, re-frame, or re-decide the inner child only adds to the created identity and keeps it alive. In other words, you must keep the identity present and functioning in order to heal it. Many therapies imply, "All parts serve a useful purpose." Quantum Psychology says, "All parts serv*ed* a useful purpose" (past tense). Why keep creating them automatically? It is time to take the *next step* and dismantle this old world view.

Last month, I was invited to give a presentation to a group of about forty psychotherapists on the East Coast. I asked the group, "Have any of you healed, or know anyone who has healed the wounded inner child?" There was *no* response. What we must find out is who is observing this inner child. In this way you—the *observer* is empowered rather than the inner child.

I said to the group, "Once you create a wounded child identity and decide to heal it by creating some other identity to say the right things to, combat it, re-assure it or champion it, you (the observer/creator) must always keep the wounded inner child identity in your psyche so that you know what it is that needs to be healed. In order to take the *next step* and go beyond the inner child you must know its' *dark side*. My Indian teacher, Nisargadatta Maharaj, would say, "First, you must know what something is in order to give it up."

The Dark Side of the Inner Child

I imagine many people would argue about the precious inner child, its value, its innocence, etc. At this time we need to understand that this "inner child" has a dark side. This inner child that some therapies are trying desperately to preserve is responsible for many present time problems.

For example, let's imagine in order to survive with Mom/Dad, you had to create a part that would *mind read* what Mom/Dad were thinking, so that you could get what you needed. The problem arises when the frozen child within your mind reads, projects and imagines what people are thinking and feeling in present time and tries to fulfill the imagining, or reacts to that imagined projection *as if* it were true.

Very often it is not true. The dark side of the inner child hypnotizes the adult into reacting to present time as if it were past time. This is what I call the dark side. It is the wounded inner child who mis-interprets, misconstrues, and misunderstands much of what it sees. To worship a precious inner child is to ignore its dark side.

Conclusion

This book will help individuals and therapists take the *next step* and (1) de-construct the inner child through understanding its strategies, and (2) return an individual to the source of his/her experience rather than referencing old experiences that no longer serve a useful purpose.

•3

Philosophy and Origins of Trance

This work represents an integration of Western Psychotherapy, Eastern Philosophy and Quantum Physics that has grown from my experience as a therapist. I have found that Western ideas such as those of Milton H. Erickson, M.D., the father of **modern** hypnosis, complement Eastern concepts of the *observer* and the understandings that developed in quantum physics, specifically by Werner Heisenberg.

Throughout this book I refer to all **states of consciousness** (other than the uninterrupted awareness of the *observer*) as a trance state. The following chapters will demonstrate that the created, time-frozen I-dentity of the inner child has certain games, strategies and thought processes. The child inside each one of us has been frozen through trauma and chaos. This can be likened to a photographer with a video camera holding his/her finger on the pause button. We are stuck with a window through which we are seeing the world, or better yet, *not* seeing the present-time world. The dark side of the wounded child I-dentity becomes our nemesis, when it shrinks the observers' present-time world, making it look like a past-time experience. In other words, the *observer* goes to sleep, and unknowingly looks through the inner child world view.

Trance can be defined as wakeful sleep. In the beginning trance occurs through a series of interactions with other people like Mom, Dad, a teacher, and even a boss, friends, husbands, wives, children, etc. The trance you designed had a purpose to maintain, protect, or support you as a child. The trance became an automatic response to other people, and developed an autonomy of its own.

Stated another way, a child relates to the family in a particular way. This is the trance the child uses in that family. As the child gets older, the trance (a) *generalizes* to all people or all women rather than Mom, so that the adult behaves like a little boy or girl around women, and (b) since it worked so well as a child, years later the *observer* puts the trance on automatic so the adult doesn't think about how to react anymore.

In this way a situation is not experienced as it is. Rather the adult, acting like a child, takes the family with him, inside, in present time, projecting it outward on others, or keeping it inside (talking to him/herself). The trance of the dark side of the inner child acts independent of present time and is the vehicle or messenger of the child within the adult. Once the inner child is frozen, it tends to shrink the focus of attention of the adult so as to produce inevitable feelings, thoughts, emotions, and for the most part, discomfort.

Trance is the major glue that holds problems together. The inner child stuck in an abusive situation might disconnect from Father, so he/she doesn't have to feel the pain of the situation. The child is frozen by the observer (you) along with the trance of disconnection. (Disconnection is called "dissociation" and will be discussed more completely in Chapter 6.)

When the *observer* fuses with the inner child, resources that could be used feel unavailable. Example: A spouse in an anger trance, throwing a tantrum at a partner, does not have the resource of remembering how much she/he loves the spouse. Rather the age-regressed inner child acts "as if" she/he were in past time with Dad. The anger trance takes the driver's seat, and the rest of the resources of present time are not there.

Any change in the trance allows the otherwise unutilized resource to become available to the *observer*. In other words, the more you know the dark side of the inner child, the freer you become to give it up. In the above example, if the trance is allowed and both people can stay in present time by seeing the tantrum as a trance of the inner child, new choices and options can emerge in their relationship.

Trances that are created by you are initially a mutual trance in the family. For example, a woman who saw me for therapy found that when she acted stupid in her family, Dad (a man) would take care of her. Her inner child had a dark side that had a "stupid" trance, which became a problem as an adult when the men she attracted treated her as though she were stupid. This process confused her. Though she was a powerful businesswoman, she was attracted to men who treated her as stupid.

What really occurred? The time-frozen little girl within her was choosing men, and was attracted to men, who were like Dad while the *observer* slept. This attraction was actually the attraction that the dark side of the inner child had. Outside of her awareness, the inner child's dark side was choosing men like Dad, which, in present time, had nothing to do with men she would be interested in.

Sometimes she would find herself going into a "stupid" trance and kick herself later for acting that way. This became the target of de-hypnosis in her therapy. Allowing the observer to de-hypnotize, observe, and awaken from a deep sleep, she saw a child identity that she had created in the past. This enabled her to emerge from a cloudy night into the open air and sunshine of choice. To de-hypnotize is to awaken to see the *you* behind the trance. You are not the child within. The child within is a re-created memory of the observer.

As mentioned above, the observer automatically recreates child-like states of consciousness from the past, as trance states in the present. It is important to understand the function and role of these trance states, which are used by the time-frozen inner child, and, to appreciate the *you* behind the inner child. My purpose is to discuss trances and the methods of moving beyond and through them so that you can experience the *you* behind those trances. My primary intent is to define trance and demonstrate how all of us, when problems arise, are in hypnotic states of mind, trance states.

This book contains many techniques of de-hypnosis for removing your "daily trance." You have created an inner child who now hypnotizes your adult into believing you are this or that. You might believe you are stupid, unattractive, unsucceessful. All of these trances come from the dark side of the child within.

Trance states are related to the flow of consciousness. They are states that are halts, distortions, and restrictions. Trance requires a *shrinking of the focus of attention* yielding symptomatic states of consciousness, or what are commonly called limitations and problems. To de-hypnotize is to shift from a trance state of shrunken or contracted feeling to the expanded experience of being an *observer/creator*, thus freeing yourself.

Over the past several years, I have continued to notice in my clinical practice that all symptoms my clients present have at least one trance associated with them. Stated another way, it has become very obvious that, in order for a problem to remain a problem, there must be at least one trance that the inner child's dark side uses like *glue* to hold the problem state together. The inner child identity sticks like glue to *you*, the observer, preventing you from experiencing present-time reality. Without the trance the symptom could not repeat itself again and again in different situations.

As I began to define the trances of the dark side of the inner child, my task with my clients became one of de-hypnosis, or awakening the *creator/observer* from a deep trance or spell of which clients were unaware.

Let me give a few, everyday examples. Anxiety is a fear of the future. A client whose presenting problem is anxiety goes into the trance of futurizing (see Chapter 5). The inner child imagines a catastrophic future and so hypnotizes the adult in present time into a fear trance. Of course, an adult hears the self-talk of the inner child's dark side, "It will never work out" (Inner Dialogue, Chapter 7), followed by an inability to see other options (Chapter 8, Blocking-Out). The dark side of the inner child might suggest to the adult that these isn't enough time, creating even more anxiety. Maybe he even imagines a bill collector taking away his house (Illusioning, Chapter 9). The presenting problem, anxiety, is full of trances, as are all problems. Most are re-creations of the dark side of the inner child. The inner child continues autonomously, with the adult experiencing past situations as present situations.

Another example is an alcoholic client who, as the session continued, began to age-regress (act younger, see Chapter 4). I insisted she keep continuous eye contact with me during the process. Quite suddenly, she couldn't see me; she fogged me out. I realized that as a child, in order for her to create distance and survive, she had to *not see* her parents. In order for her problem (alcoholism) to continue, the dark side of the inner child had to maintain a trance, changing her relationship to the present-time world. She had to change from self-to-the-world in present time to a trance, child-to-parents in past time.

Although she fogged out her parents' drinking, in order *to not see it*, another *dissociated part* of her saw it. Although part of her was hiding in the fog, another part saw the drinking. This is the power of dissociation in action. The *observer/creator* of the trance state *holds* and takes a picture of the fog and the drinking. Years later, the child within the adult had two sides: fogger/drinker.

More simply put, the observer took a picture of the little girl watching her parents drinking. To handle that, the little girl *fogged out* her parents drinking so she did not have to experience what was occurring. By having her hold eye contact with me in the therapeutic process, she went into the little girl within the adult who had fogged out to survive. What "popped up " was the memory of her parents drinking (the other side of the inner child). As will be discussed later, the processes by which I got her to stop fogging out de-hypnotized her, so in her life she no longer fogged out automatically, and was no longer in denial about her parents drinking.

The glue which held the drinking was the trance I call "blocking out," or not seeing what is there. I began to stop the blocking by suggesting that the child within see transparency, opaqueness, translucency, colors in the fog. (See "Blocking Out" Chapter 8.)

Since the dark side of the inner child could no longer follow the path of blocking out as part of her "frozen pattern," she could no longer continue the child-like drinking trance in present time.

As I watch my clients closely, I note the trances their inner child is using, as the glue that holds their problems. As each trance is released, the problem loses the ability to repeat itself.

It is my purpose to outline in this book many of the concepts and ideas that have come clear to me over the past 20 years working with clients, so that people can take the *next step*; de-hypnotize their own inner child, put it to rest, and move on in their lives. I am proposing a model of **"recovered,"** rather than "in recovery" for a lifetime. By understanding the dark side of the inner child and the trances the inner child uses, there is an opportunity to identify problem trance states and de-hypnotize from unwanted behaviors, emotions, or feelings.

Conclusion

Understanding that trances are the glue of problems affords an opportunity to explore, define, and spot your own trances and the trances of others. This book is a practical guide for self-explorers to handle their trances and the dark side of the inner child.

The chapters that follow explore in depth 10 typical trances lived and invoked by the inner child.

Age Regression: Acting Younger Than You Are

I was dreaming of the past
and my heart was beating fast,
I began to lose control
I began to lose control...

I was feeling insecure
You don't love me anymore
I was shivering inside
I was shivering inside

I didn't mean to hurt you
I'm sorry that I made you cry
I didn't mean to hurt
I'm just a jealous guy.

"Jealous Guy," John Lennon

In this song from the *Imagine* album, Lennon talks of two trances. First, he shifted from being an adult in present time to being a wounded child in past time. Secondly, he didn't lose control; rather, he became the inner child who was frozen, lost control and was shivering, scared, and jealous. Lennon could have called the song "Jealous Wounded Child" rather than "Jealous Guy", because, in order to feel the feelings, he had to become the inner child (dreaming of the past) and age regress (become younger than he was).

Isn't this a familiar process for us all? Our partner looks a certain way, and suddenly we are drenched in a sea of emotions. This is the dark side of the inner child, an automatic response pattern, which overwhelms us, making the present look like the past.

Age regression, or feeling younger than you are, is the cornerstone of the wounded child identity. Here, the *observer* takes a picture of a traumatic incident and holds that picture (memory) of this little child going through a trauma. The picture records the look, the pain, the feelings. Whenever anything resembles the picture, the dark side of the inner child takes over, reproducing memories and feelings that have little to do with present time reality. In short, the dark side of the inner child projects the past incident onto the present situation.

Age regression is the most widely experienced trance and relates directly to a time frozen experience that was uncomfortable and too confusing or chaotic for the child to experience and integrate completely; hence, the observer resisted the experience, causing the memory of what occurred to freeze. This experience of being "stuck" in a past place or point in one's personal history is the inner child's stuckness, not the present-time adult. This is why, as an adult, you say, feel, or react in certain ways out of your control and don't understand why. You relate to the world through the inner child identity, which creates the parameters for future interpersonal limitation. In other words, seeing our present-time relationship through the past-time window of the inner child limits our view, resources, emotional parameters, and our decisions.

Let's take an example of a mother who wants her child to "please her." Asking a child to please Mom in order to get love, attention, and approval can be more traumatic for the child than might normally be appreciated. Asking a child to give up what they want, or even to "give-up themselves" to please Mom, and hence survive, is asking a child to give up an internal need. In the confusion and chaos of determining how to survive, the *observer* creates a pleasing-child identity.

Throughout the book, I break down the word identity to *I*-dentity, to emphasize how the adult in present time becomes an *I*-dentity in past time. Calling the memory "*I*" creates a separate *I*-dentity (This will be discussed further in Chapter 6). In this case, however, the child gives up himself and represses his inner wants or desires. In fact in many cases of co-dependency, the pleasing aspect of the child is covered by a layer of rage.

In this example, the inner-child pleaser created by the *observer* also has its opposite, an angry dark side which the pleaser is masking. After all, wouldn't you get angry if you had to please to get love? Often times clients I work with have a continual low-grade anger or irritation, which they blame on the world. When a client presents me with, "I am continually angry at the world," I ask her, " What need do you have that is unmet?" Frustration and anger is caused by not getting what you need or want. Often times we get angry and blame the outer world rather than asking ourselves, "What do I want that I am not getting?"

This interrupts the inner child's anger and blaming of the outside world, by forcing the adult to look at what need he has that isn't being met, acknowledged or mentioned.

Blaming

There is such a relief in knowing who's to blame. If you are suffering, someone must be responsible....Blaming often involves making someone responsible for choices and decisions that are actually your own responsibility. In blame systems (trances), somebody is always doing it to you, and you have no responsibility to assert your needs, say no, or go elsewhere for what you want. (McKay, 1981:23)

Of course getting a person to directly ask for what she wants from her partner or spouse is difficult, because the dark side of the wounded inner child wants to get without asking. Asking is too vulnerable, too risky, because the child was punished for being open. Often times, parents give suggestions like, "Who do you think you are?" "Do you think money grows on trees." In India (see Chapter 14, "Spiritualization") they believe that saying what you want or even *wanting* is the source of all human problems. In many situations, the child learns how to get what is wanted not by asking directly, but rather by acting indirectly. This is often *modeled* by Mom and Dad, who show the child how to get what is wanted without asking. The parents can *model* this manipulation, and years later the child within the adult gets angry at a spouse because the spouse doesn't "mind read" the inner child's signals. Complaints in a relationship occur often times because the spouse doesn't know what is wanted, since it wasn't asked for.

I once had a client who was working on his relationship with his mother. I asked, "What do you want from her?" The inner child responded, "I wanted her to give me everything I wanted, whenever I wanted it, without having to ask." The adult saw how out of line the inner child's demand was and was able to let it go.

Cutting off our feelings is traumatic. Often the child has to repress or pretend his own wishes or desires are not important. Years later, he doesn't even know what he wants. Noted psychiatrist Dr. Wilhelm Reich, in his book *The Murder of Christ*, likens one's natural life force or energy to Christ. Reich suggests that a parent, in trying to get a child to conform and give up feelings or needs, "kills" the natural life force of the child. Reich calls this the "emotional plague." Reich states that as your life force is killed or repressed, so you will force others to repress natural energy and emotional energy. Stated more simply, the degree to which your life force was repressed or killed by another is the same degree to which you will try to repress or kill another's life force.

In recent years the ancient healing system of acupuncture, long acknowledged in Asia, has gained popularity in the West. Why? We are beginning to believe, like Reich, that disease is caused by blocking the natural flow of energy in the body.

As an example, a woman who is treated in her family as unintelligent might experience this as painful and try hard to fight against it. Inside, her frozen inner child continues to create the trance, "I'm not smart." This seems to occur in individuals frequently. Often times, physical symptoms like migraine headaches, ulcers, and colitis accompany these emotional problems. After all, it takes a lot of energy to hold back the natural life force of the body. Interestingly enough, the word "emotion" can be broken down into "e" meaning outward, and "motion", hence, outward motion. Psychologically and physically, an interruption in outward motion can cause both psychological and physical disease.

As another example, let's imagine a child who has a powerful energy motion toward Mom. Mom labels that energy "anger" and "thwarts it" either by words, punishment or withdrawal of love. That outward flow of energy, which is now labeled "anger" must go somewhere. Where does it go? The child puts it back on herself creating self-anger, self-hatred, guilt and/or depression. I recently saw a client who got sore throats whenever he felt anger. As we began to focus on his throat, an image of Dad emerged. When I asked him to express his anger at Dad, he could barely talk. I asked him, "What would you like to say to Dad?" He replied, "I'd like to strangle him." When I asked him to reach out and do it (in his mind), his throat contracted, and he had an urge to strangle himself. Here we see someone unable to express the outward motion toward Dad and, instead, turning it against himself and "strangling" himself. The result: chronic sore throats.

In life when a problem appears, it often has a "feeling younger" quality to it that repeats itself not only at an emotional and physical level but also at a cognitive level. It can be presupposed that any problem contains an element of age regression (acting younger than you are), which is the *signal* that the inner child has taken over.

As in all trances and identities, the age-regressed inner child effects the adult in present time. What is meant by this is that the *observer* freezes the inner-child identity and relates to the present-time world through this window. Interestingly enough, that "fear" feels frozen and cold, a major complaint of many clients. In other words the *observer* freezes the memory by using fear. Fear, therefore, becomes the vehicle used by the *observer* to freeze the natural flow of a memory.

The inner child relates child-to-adult in past time, rather than self-to-other in present time. For example, I was working with a

divorced woman, who said that her husband was constantly imagining she was a bitch. No matter what she did to prove otherwise, he
continued to claim this was so. One day over lunch, she looked into
his eyes and noticed a film covering his eyes. He had moved from
a present-time interaction (self-to-wife) to an inner child trance
(child-to-Mom) and he was watching some past picture of mom,
that he overlaid on his wife in present time.

This process, moving into the inner child, explains why we
often feel alone in relationships. We move from self-to-other in
present time, to child-to-parents in past time. The inner child
becomes the hypnotist making suggestions to the present-time
adult, who is the subject. In doing this, we lose our connection with
the other person and the present world and hence feel lonely,
misunderstood, and alienated.

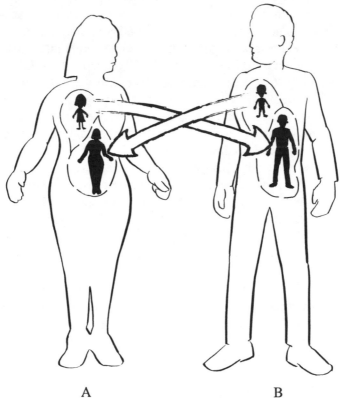

A   B

Illustration #2

In illustration #2 we see the inner child of person B hypnotizing the internalized parent in person A. Interestingly, the inner child of person A is hypnotizing the parent of person B. This is *trance-*ference, and counter *trance*-ference, and is the cornerstone of problem states that occur in relationships.

In the former example, where the woman goes into the "I'm not smart enough" a inner child trance, she probably will pick a man who treats her that way. This mutual inner child trance between her and her husband possibly might be a re-creation of both her inner child and his inner-child family trance. (See Illustration 2.) The inner child's trance becomes frozen or created by a series of interpersonal interactions in the family, which take over individual experiences of NOW. In essence, both husband and wife become their age-regressed inner-child identity and project the parent on the other person, thus losing their present-time relationship.

Age regression describes the process an adult goes through as he becomes the inner child. This creates blind spots. A relationship cannot work if neither person is in present time. Interactions are "time frozen," because NOW is experienced as if it were a prior time. Consequently, behavior appears as if it were now, while actually a person is acting as if he were a child or adolescent in his family.

The Task

1. Identify when you become or feel younger than you are.
2. Notice when it occurs and what triggers it.
3. Notice where in your physical or mental space the inner child resides. For example, is the inner child in your mental space, physical body, both?
4. Watch and observe the inner child identity.
5. Observe and take responsibility for the created inner child identity.

6. Notice that you are the *observer* and creator of the inner child identity window you are looking through.

7. Learn to stop creating the inner child identity as a window to view present reality.

Age regression is a trance, understood as the basic process during which the observer moves from present time to a frozen picture of a child interacting with an adult in past time. The *observer* takes that past-time picture and overlays or trance-fers it on top of present time experiences. The *observer* sees the world through the eyes of the dark side of the inner child by overlaying what is actually occurring. Breaking this habit de-hypnotizes the *observer* and places the memory (picture) back in linear time. As long as the memory and the inner child are out of control, they will "pop up" on their own, outside the awareness of the adult.

For example, let's say there is an *observer* observing a small girl in 1950. The little girl gets molested by Uncle Henry. At the time, the *observer* cannot understand what is occurring and feels chaos or confusion. In that chaos, the *observer* "freezes the action of the film," and to protect the (little girl), the *observer* decides, "Don't trust men or this will happen again," or "Remember this so it won't happen again." In 1993, the 42 year old woman has a wounded inner child that pops up when John tries to be intimate. The observer trance-fers the past occurrence with Uncle Henry in 1950 to the present one with John. The present-day woman age regresses and becomes the wounded child who freezes, feels scared, and may or may not know why. De-hypnosis undoes the trance of the past so the memory that pops up can get placed in the background as a memory, rather than *trance*-ferred over present-time reality, as a foreground.

In this case the *observer* takes a picture of the little girl being molested and the perpetrator (Uncle Henry). Both parts reside within the inner child, i.e., victim and perpetrator. These two parts of the inner child become the world view of men even years later. Hence the perpetrator gets *trance*-ferred on men and the victim feels scared, or the victim gets *trance*-ferred on a child and the perpetrator-part of the inner child takes over and abuses. It is the perpetrator-part of the inner child that molests children; that is why the research demonstrates that almost all child molesters were molested as children. Let me give another example.

Recently, I was working with a client who complained how much she hated herself, and how she heard a voice inside her head saying, "You're bad," "You deserve to be punished," and "I hate you." We discovered that as a child she was physically abused by her stepfather who would say **precisely** these things to her. What occurred was that the *observer* took a picture of the beaten child and the stepfather. Both lived inside of her, and she would hear the voices inside of her saying, "You're bad," "You deserve to be punished," and "I hate you." This part of the inner child had fused and *become* the perpetrator. So the perpetrator's voice (hypnotic suggestion) had become part of the inner child's dark side.

These voices and the ensuing poor self-esteem was a past- time trance, which came from the perpetrator. Once the inner child fuses with the voice, even years later, the perpetrator lives within the adult as an inner child identity, giving the adult outrageous suggestions. This will be discussed in greater detail in Chapter 7, "Inner Dialogue". Suffice to say for now that a critical issue in the treatment of incest is the fusion with the perpetrator. (See Illustration 3, page 34) It is freezing the memory and the resistance to the chaos of the situation that causes the memory to pop up on its own and become foreground of its own volition. **De-hypnosis allows the memory to become background, allowing present time to be foreground.**

Discovering your inner child and the trance that holds problems in place is crucial. Then the experience can be worked with so that responsibility can shift to the observer, the creator of the inner child. Your task is to observe and appreciate your inner child's trance, that you probably would have called your problem or symptom. Since the trance was used as a survival mechanism in your family of origin, we call it a "family trance" because you as a child were the subject and your parents the hypnotists. Individuals have learned to survive by utilizing trance skills in their families. Children who don't obey the family trance can be labeled "bad" or "troublemakers." People go into trances not knowing, for instance, that they are acting like a child. This is the process of age regression.

Here is another example. The little girl who sits on Daddy's lap and learns how to "be cute" so Daddy will buy her a new dress, is that same little girl who is sitting on Hubby's lap being cute so that she gets what she wants. These are exactly the same inner-child trance experiences. The trance of age regression allows that phenomenon, the present-time adult becoming a past-time child, to manifest itself in the present.

You construct your experience using the process of age regression by altering subjectively how you experience the present. The job is to awaken from your dream shifting, from being the child in

CHILD VICTIM

PERPETRATOR (HYPNOTIST)

Illustration #3

past time, to being the *observer/creator* of your experience in present time. Once awakened from the inner child's trance, resources of the present become available to you which were *not* available to the child.

When the trance is unglued, present-time problems lose power. The last trance example, called "being cute," had become a permanent fixture of her experience. Her trance worked as a survival mechanism. In order to survive the childhood environment, she had developed a trance experience, called "being cute." It worked in that situation, and certain episodes in her present-time adult environment triggered the child within to hypnotize the adult in present time.

The Next Step
Working with Age Regression

Remember.

Re-member. To *re*-member is to become a *member* of present time reality.

When handling age-regressed states completely and totally, allow the resisted experience to unfold. In other words, you need to look at whatever chaos (trauma) or memory caused the observer to "stop action" or push "pause" on the film. It was the resistance to looking at what was occurring that placed the movie on "hold," to be reviewed again, and again, and again.

Step I: Identify the trance.

The most important step in getting out of an inner child trance is to recognize you're in it. Richard Alpert (Ram Dass) would say, "In order to get out of a jail, first you must realize you're in one." (Ram Dass, *The Only Dance There Is*) The fact is, that 90% of the process is realizing that there is a "child inside" operating. Why? Because, you must step out of the trance of the inner child just to notice or be aware that you are age-regressing as an adult. By *noticing* and observing the aged-regressed child, you are being the *observer*, the first crucial step.

Step II: Answer the following questions and make a list of your answers.

Question 1: *location*. Notice where the inner-child Identity is located in the physical body or in mental space?

Question 2: *Self-esteem*. By fusing with this Identity, does your perspective of yourself change? How?

Question 3: *World View*. By fusing with this Identity, is your perception of the world changing? How?

Question 4: Does this identity have any emotions or feelings associated with it? Which ones?

Step III:

Now that we are clearer about this inner child Identity, ask the Identity two more questions, and write down your answers. Keep asking the questions until nothing else pops up.

Question 1. What are you, the inner child identity, resisting knowing about yourself?

Question 2. What are you, the inner child identity, resisting experiencing?

Allow the answers to come from the inner-child Identity, and write them down.

Step IV: Homework.

Note your answers, and this week begin to observe how often you take on and become this Identity.

Step V:

Finally, give the identity a name, like, loser, victim, manipulator. Each time it pops up for you, or you notice you are fused with it internally, call its name e.g., victim, loser. This will help you to de-fuse and unfuse with the inner child, thus allowing you to become the *observer* in present time.*

Conclusion

Being able to identify both sides of the inner child's trance allows us to *observe* its workings. It is the self-observation of the workings of the inner child that adds *awareness*. Awareness is the solvent for the glue of the automatic trance states of the child within the adult. In order to give something up, you must first know what it is. These exercises, when applied, give us the awareness that is needed to know the workings of this inner-child Identity so we can give it up and return to the present-time world.

---

*This approach of giving subpersonalities a name was developed in *Psychosynthesies* by Roberto Assagioli.

•5

Futurizing

Life is what happens to you, while you're busy making other plans.

"Beautiful Boy," John Lennon

In John Lennon's classic song "Beautiful Boy," Lennon describes a phenomenon that we all experience: our bodies being in present time, but our minds moving into the future. "Futurizing" describes this process, whether it be planning for the future, imaging a catastrophe in the future, imagining a pleasant outcome in the future, or just imagining talking with someone in the future. This trance comes from the dark side of the time-frozen inner child and it keeps us out of present-time reality.

In the immortal classic by H.G. Wells, *The Time Machine*, a person is able to go forward or backward in time. The problem with futurizing is 1) travel is not in "real time" but in imagined time, and (2) in the time machine, a switch gives the operator choice, with automatic futurizing, there is no choice. A person finds himself in the future. Frequently, clients complain of anxiety, (fear of the future). All too often, this fear of the future is actually fear of an imagined future.

For example, I am in a relationship and feel "in love." I go away for business for a week and imagine my girlfriend having an affair. As the fantasy continues, I futurize myself coming home several days later, moving to my own apartment and being alone and unhappy. The odd part about futurizing is that I feel the pain of the imagined situation *right now*, even though it is a fantasy of a catastrophic future.

1. Catastrophizing

In the cognitive therapy of Albert Ellis, he categorizes one style of futurizing: catastrophizing.

"Catastrophic thoughts often start with the words what if. *What if* my daughter gets pregnant? *What if* I lose my job? *What if* I get sick and can't work?" (McKay, 1981:21)

Catastrophizing, which is one style of futurizing, takes place when a person projects herself into the future and imagines a catastrophic outcome. As mentioned earlier, the complaint of anxiety is imagining a catastrophic outcome and experiencing distress now. This trance of the dark side of the inner child takes place as the child sees trauma in his life. The child *assumes* that this is how life will always be. As an adult, the child within the adult continually "pops-up" catastrophies and thinks they are real. The result is pain and suffering in present time. Here, past catastrophies are projected into the future.

2. Fantasizing

In this style of the futurizing trance, the child imagines a pleasant outcome in the future. The pleasant imagined outcome helps protect the child from the distressing, ongoing interactions in the family. For example, a child imagines herself waiting "for her ship to come in," or imagines her talent being "discovered," or fantasizes a time when she will be "taken care of." Problems arise when the child within the adult stays "stuck" and continues to imagine the unrealistic idealized future. A woman I once saw for therapy was in a relationship with a man for years and was always frustrated. She wanted him to take care of her. She felt frustrated because, outside of her awareness, the dark side of the inner child was hypnotizing the present-time adult, making her believe that this was supposed to happen—hence the adult in present time felt frustrated and angry at her partner for not taking care of her.

The important thing to note is that with each style of futurizing the adult shifts from a present-time reality, to the inner-child reality that *trance*-fers the past to the future. In futurizing, so strong is the trance of the inner child that the adult believes the future is the past.

Why do these "trances" occur? A child in a stressful situation often feels confused, overwhelmed, crazy or chaotic. In that chaos, the observer creates a fantasy that helps dissipate the feeling of chaos.

For example, I was seeing a woman for therapy who, as a little girl, had to take care of her physically ill Dad. She felt trapped. Her survival mechanism was to imagine a wonderful man taking her away from all of this, thus the feelings of being overwhelmed dissipated.

A gentleman I was seeing for therapy, had lived as a small boy in a poverty-stricken situation. To handle that, he created a fantasy of money coming to him. His distress would subside.

In both cases, fantasizing worked for the child to handle the situation. Problems arose however when the child within became automatic and time-frozen. When the woman came for therapy, she had a history of picking men she wanted to have take care of her. She never developed a career, and these men did not want to take care of her. She came to my office lamenting, very needy, having driven men away, and without a relationship.

The child within the man, in the latter example, was continually obsessing about not having enough money. Instead of working to make a living, he would fantasize money coming to him. The inner child within the man began to develop "New Age" philosophies that believe visualizing money makes it come. (See Chapter 14, Spiritualization.) When he came to see me, he was broke, married, living in a trailer, not working, selling possessions for food.

Such is the power of the fantasizing trance of "futurizing". The dark side of the inner child alleviates emotional stress but functions without feedback from the real world. The child within the adult thinks the fantasy is reality. It's not that the inner child is wrong or bad, but just that what worked at ages two through six does not work at age 36.

At first, futurizing is dependent on the events of early life. Problems arise when futurizing becomes autonomous, has a life of its own. It acts on its own, independently, being cut adrift from its original source, the family. In this way fantasies arise on their own, and people live life fantasizing about the future, rather than experiencing "now."

Another trance form associated with futurizing occurs when the individual creates self-talk, an internal dialogue (see Chapter 7, Inner Dialogue). "I never get what I want," is an example. Not only is *now* catastrophic for the child, but the future also is imagined as catastrophic. This orientation is a combination of age regression, in which the past is "fixed," but also the past pain is trance-fered to the future. This "time-frozen pattern" is also an age regression since the anxiety trance comes from the dark side of the child within, *not* from the adult in present time. In present time the adult has many resources available. It is the child within that feels there are no resources. The adult feels the child trance as real and so experiences anxiety. The past pain stays alive as an experience in the present, and as a projected, imagined future. In this state there is only frozen past time overlayed on present or future time. A negative association with the experience of the past is created and re-enacted many times without seeing *now*.

Unfortunately for the present time adult, the inner child is so good at hypnotizing the adult, that the adult does not know that he is seeing the future, or past as the present. Recently, I was working with a therapist as a client who was upset and angry with a married couple he was working with. He complained angrily, "Why is he living with this abusive woman." Through therapy, he realized that his inner child had trance-ferred his past-time parents on this married couple. His inner child hypnotized my client, who was a family therapist, into treating the man as his mother and the woman as his father. He realized, as he observed the inner child, that in many of his relationships, his age-regressed inner child trance-fered the past Mom and Dad on present-time people. This is more common than therapists realize. For many years I was trained as a family therapist. As I watched other family therapists work, I would watch them, (through the one-way miror) age-regress and feel powerless to help a couple or family. This is the power of age-regression. Even trained family therapists have a dark side of an inner child in them. If, while giving therapy, the family who is receiving therapy activates the therapist's inner child, the therapist age-regresses and feels powerless to help the family. This is exactly how the therapist felt as a child—powerless to help their family. This is why the family trance is so powerful, and often times why some family therapists work with a co-therapist in the room. Hopefully, one of them will stay in present time and not age-regress.

Futurizing is experienced by people who are in a daily state of free-floating anxiety. Futurizing has elements of inner dialogues and age regression. The goal is to work and emancipate yourself from the child's trance, and dehypnotize yourself, to resolve the anxiety.

Trances of the inner child are born of chaos, so how could a child born of chaos produce anything else but chaos? The inner child looks through a window of chaos and trys to rectify it through trance, creating even more present-time chaos.

An example is a little girl or boy who grows up in a dysfunctional family. These children will read and identify with a story like Horatio Alger, an impoverished child that became rich and successful. Another example is the girl who grows up with the classic "Cinderella" complex. Here the observer creates the state; "Everything is so awful that some day Prince Charming is going to take me away from all this." These trance systems helped the child handle the situation. When reality is threatening, he/she imagines a more pleasant, successful future.

In my forthcoming book, *The Tao of Chaos*, we will explore the resistance to chaos as precluding development of all systems.

A woman came to see me because she was experiencing anxiety from the fact that in two weeks her divorce would be final. The dark side of the child within her suffered anxiety and created a catastrophic future in the divorce property settlement. I suggested she notice where in her body the child within lived. Often times the child within gets frozen in areas of the body causing tightness in the jaw, chest, stomach, pelvis and in extreme cases a feeling of paralysis. As mentioned earlier and emphasized in my former book *Trances People Live: Healing Approaches in Quantum Psychology,* trances require a tightening of the muscles of the body and a holding of the breath.

In this example, I asked her to *intentionally* create the child living in her stomach by placing the fear and inner voices inside. I asked her to continue creating the fear and accompanying fantasies. I asked her, "Tell me the difference between you *(the observer)* and the inner child." She responded, "Well, I can observe the inner child." I asked her to keep creating the inner child and the catastrophizing. After creating it *intentionally*, she took charge of the panicked inner child and realized that she was the *observer/creator* of it, hence she could stop creating it.

The most important task of the observer is to create the inner child intentionally. This is the reason noted physicist John Wheeler changed the word observer in physics to the word *participator*. Why? Because the *observer* not only observes; the *observer* also *participates* in the creation of internal subjective reality.

The *intentional* creation of the experience makes it possible to choose. You awaken the observer to its creative aspect by asking the observer to create *intentionally and knowingly*, that which they are creating *unknowingly*. The observer has been sleeping and is hypnotized. By having the observer create his own trance, the *observer* awakens to its creative aspect.

3. *Planning*

"Planning" is a form of futurizing that occurs when the child cannot tell her parents how she feels. She imagines a time in the future when she tells her parents how she feels and the parents understand and admit they were wrong.

I saw a very famous writer in Santa Cruz, who wrote a book putting his famous father down. He built a case, in a lecture I attended, showing how he was good and Dad was bad. What was extraordinary was that, at the end of the story, Dad admits he was wrong and the son was right, and the audience exploded in applause. Why? Many people hold this trance.

Another style of planning takes place when a child cannot tell his parents how he feels so he *plans* ways to spite or get even with his parents in the future. This is a "winning by losing" trance, and here I often ask clients to fill in the blanks:

1. I spite you by _____.
2. I get even with you by _____.

3. I win by losing by _____.
4. I'll show you. I won't _____.
5. I'll show you. I will _____.

These questions make the implicit explicit and reveal this classic masochistic trance of the dark side of the inner child.

4. *The Explainer*

I call this trance "play it again, Sam," because a friend of mine planned conversations, explanations, or justifications in the future with people. Whenever he noticed this occurring, he would say, "Here we go again, tape loop 98.74, play it again."

In this case, the child might have done something wrong or knows it will be punished in the future, based on past experience. So the dark side of the inner child plans a justification in the future. The child practices arguments for and against, like an attorney making an appeal. Catastrophizing can accompany this, so the guillotine (heavy punishment from the parents) pushes the justifier even further. The trance is an imagined future; the child within has a justifier trance, continually explaining and justifying actions, reactions, emotions and the basic "whys" of life. The justifier gets justice or doesn't, but the trance of imagining catastrophe (and counter-punching the impending doom with a justification in the future) continues, even as the adult grows older.

5. *Fallacy of Fairness*

In cognitive therapy, there is a thinking distortion called "fallacy of fairness."

"This distorted thinking style hinges on the application of legal and contractual rules to the vagaries of interpersonal relations. The trouble is that two people seldom agree on what *fairness* is, and there is no court or final arbitrator to help them. *Fairness* is a subjective assessment of how much of what one expected, needed, or hoped for has been provided by the temptingly self-serving, that each person gets locked into his or her own point of view.

The fallacy of fairness is often expressed in conditional assumptions: If he loved me, he'd do ... If he loved me, he'd help me to orgasm ... If this was a real marriage, she'd hike with me and learn to like it ... If he cared at all, he'd come home right after work... If they valued my work here, they'd get me a nicer desk.

It is tempting to make assumptions about how things would change if people were *fair* or *really* valued you. But other people hardly see it that way and you end up causing yourself a lot of pain." (McKay 1981:22)

Where do These Trances and Thinking Styles Come From?

Trances and thinking styles can come from the *observer* taking a picture of mom's and dad's behavior, and using it as a model for the future. The *observer* creates an inner child that is a duplicate of the parents. The *observer* then goes to sleep and the created inner child walks like, talks like, acts like, sounds like, and even feels the same as the parents feel toward life. This is why so often, if you have children, you act and talk to your children, just as your mother or father acted or talked to you.

In the fallacy of fairness, a certain value system is generally absorbed by the child from Mom, Dad, or both, which teaches the child what is fair. For example, Mom and Dad had an unspoken agreement that Dad works and Mom stays home with the kids. This trade-off is thought of as "fair." If Mom wants to go visit her sister for a few days, Dad says, "That's not fair." Let's say Mom and Dad pay for your schooling, and you drop out. Mom and Dad say, "That isn't fair because, after all, we paid for you." Fair is a term that is relative to a particular position and value system. So the observer learns what is fair through modeling, and learning how to act and feel, e.g., depressed, betrayed, when this implicit contract of fairness is not carried out.

There used to be a workshop in Los Angeles in the mid-1970's called, "If you loved me you would _____." It recognized that problems arise when an angry or depressed child within the adult assumes unstated contracts of fairness, without checking it out. The emotional state of the adult is the result of the child within duplicating his family's reaction to the betrayal of fairness.

The Next Step
Handling Futurizing

Step I: Notice when the inner child is futurizing.

Step II: Identify the brand of futurizing the inner child is creating.

1. Catastrophizing
2. Fantasizing
3. Planning
4. The Explainer/Justifier
5. Fallacy of Fairness

Step III: Notice where in your body the inner child lives by noticing areas of tension or tightness.

For Catastrophizing:
Dialogue with the inner child.

Ask the inner child these questions and write down all of your answers. *Make sure the answers come from the inner child—not the adult figuring out what the inner child might say.*

1. What incident do you (the inner child) remember that caused this catastrophizing? Write down your answers.
2. What incident do you (the inner child) not know about, that might have caused this catastrophizing?
3. What catastrophic incident in the past might you (the inner child) be projecting into the future?
4. "What incident do you (the inner child) not know about that might cause this projection of a catastrophic past into future?
5. Are you (the inner child) resisting this knowing and experience?

6. Intentionally resist the experience.
7. Intentionally have the experience.
8. Intentionally create both the experience and the resistance.
9. Notice you are the *observer/creator* of the experience.

For Fantasizing
Write down your answers.

1. Ask the inner child, "What happened in the past that you (the inner child) are resisting?"
2. Ask the inner child, "What incident do you not know about that may have happened in the past, that caused this fantasizing of the future?"
3. Ask the inner child, "Are you resisting this knowing and experience?"
4. Intentionally resist the experience.
5. Intentionally have the experience.
6. Intentionally create the experience and resistance.
7. Notice you are the *observer/creator* of the experience.

For Planning
Write down your answers.

1. Ask the inner child, "What happened in the past that you are projecting in the future?"
2. Ask the inner child, "What may have happened in the past that I do not know about, that caused this projection of past into future?"
3. Are you (the inner child) resisting this knowing and experience?
4. Intentionally resist the experience.
5. Intentionally have the experience.
6. Intentionally create the experience and the resistance.
7. Notice you are the *observer/creator* of the experience.

For The Explainer (Justifier)

1. Ask the inner child, "What incident may have happened in the past that caused you to justify yourself?"

2. Ask the inner child, "What incident may have happened in the past that you do not know about that caused this projection of past justifications into future?"
3. Ask the inner child, "Are you resisting this knowing and experience?"
4. Intentionally resist the experience.
5. Intentionally have the experience.
6. Intentionally create the experience and the resistance.
7. Notice you are the *observer/creator* of the experience.

For the Fallacy of Fairness

1. Notice when the inner child is in the fallacy of fairness.
2. Whose (Mom/Dad) value system and feelings (Mom or Dad) did your inner child take on?
3. Be the observer of the Mom/Dad value system that yields particular feelings.
4. See the feelings as coming from Mom/Dad.
5. Create the feelings and voices several times.
6. Notice you are the *observer/creator* of the experience.

Conclusion

With all trances of the inner child, the key solvent to the process is *awareness*. Remember:

1. You *(the observer)* are in the inner child's trance.
2. Notice where in your body the inner child is located.
3. Notice the brand of trance and thinking style involved.
4. Observe and create them until you *(the observer)* can take responsibility for the dark side of the inner child.

Awareness becomes the major solvent for the glue of futurizing. Once awareness is added, the *observer/creator* (you) are free to stop automatically creating the problem again and again, unknowingly.

•6

Dis-connection: Feeling Separate From Yourself or Others

Dis-connection is a trance that the *observer* creates which enables the child to disconnect from uncomfortable situations. Commonly called dissociation in psychology, the trance of disconnection occurs when a child is unable to handle the family and so the *observer* creates a disconnection. Disconnection can be experienced as spacing out, or feeling like you're not there. Problems arise when the *observer* sleeps and the child within the adult disconnects and goes into a disconnection trance *automatically*.

Disconnection is a trance that can be experienced in several styles:

1. *Not Owning Trance*

An *observer* might disconnect a child in a stressful family situation. The *observer* disconnects the child from parts of his or her self. For example, if a child is not allowed to show affection, the *observer* might disconnect the child from that particular feeling. Years later, the inner child may experience a disconnection-from-intimacy trance. If a child is not allowed to get angry, the *observer* disconnects the child from that feeling. Years later, the angry part erupts from the frozen child, but when asked, "Are you angry," the person replies from the adult's point of view, "Who me, angry? Of course not. I never get angry." The adult experience is that he never gets angry. It is some disconnected part that gets angry and, if he could get rid of it, everything would be fine.

2. *Disappearing*

In a dysfunctional family a child might leave, or disappear, and experience his or her self as "not here." To protect a child of alcoholic parents the *observer* either inwardly or outwardly makes the child feel like he disappears and, hence, the child feels invisible.

This disappearing trance can create huge problems in relationships, particularly in the area of intimacy. She literally disappears, going nowhere, or she might imagine herself someplace else, e.g., the beach, in the mountains, anything to avoid present time. What makes this trance interesting is that the body smiles, nods, carries on a conversation, yet no one is home. Often people don't remember what was told them, or what they agreed to. (See Chapter 12, Amnesia)

Disconnection is often used in later years to develop a "spiritual practice." Meditation can actually be *medication*, dulling, numbing or not owning one's experience. The difference between real observation and disconnection is simple. If you are *free* to experience an emotion like anger, and *free not* to, then you are in pure observation and truly meditating. If you cannot or will not experience your feelings but have to disconnect from them under the guise of spirituality, you might be using meditation as *medication* and a spiritual philosophy to re-enforce your disconnection.* Furthermore, to protect the child during a trauma an *observer* might create a dissociative state, which, often times, protects the child from the pain of the trauma. Meditation is used as *medication*. The person goes into a dissociative trance and thinks its meditation because

---

*This is elaborated upon in *Quantum Consciousness* by Stephen H. Wolinsky, "*Is it Dissociation or Observation?*", pg. 30, Bramble Books, CT, 1993.

they feel peaceful and calm. In reality, however, this dissociative trance hides the trauma. The strategy of the *observer* creating dissociative trances to protect the child *appears*, like meditation, but is only a combination of amnesia and numbing-out called dissociation.

I had a psychiatrist friend, who, because he couldn't feel, imagined he was spiritual. He developed anorexia (not eating) and called it "fasting." As this escalated, he began using enemas under the spiritual label of "purification."

The disconnection of the inner child within the adult can become so strong that in order not to feel, any means is adopted, even meditation or using spirituality as *medication*. (See Chapter 14, Spiritualization)

3. *I Am Not My Body Trance*:

A particular body part, due to parental or family suggestions, may be experienced as "not me." For example, frequently in this culture, both men and women are forced to dis-connect from sexual feelings. Men often give their penis a name, as if it has a life of its own. Comedian Robin Williams calls his penis "Mr. Happy."

This disconnection trance has created far-reaching sexual disconnections that produce many relationship problems. Often, this manifests in cases of frigidity in women, impotence or premature ejaculation in men. If a man disconnects from his penis, he may either not feel sexual sensations enough to have an erection, or fixate his entire attention on his penis, losing the rest of his body and prematurely ejaculate. A women who cannot have an orgasm may have disconnected from her own genitals. Often, suffering from these sexual disconnections occurs during childhood sexual abuse; this will be discussed in greater depth in Chapter 13, Sensory Distortion, and Chapter 14, Spiritualization.

In more subtle instances, a child may experience his or her mouth as being separate from his or her self. The child might have had to respond to parents (play their game) to such an extent that the child is always paying *lip service* and is not experiencing his or her mouth or words as coming from his or her self. These automatic head nods, smiles, or "pretends," hide the *observer* behind the trance. The *observer* is protecting the child's true feelings. Years later at work or in relationships, the inner child within the adult will automatically *play the game* and go into a disconnection-from-self trance.

I once had a man come into a session who had a Ph.D. in Chemistry from Harvard. He complained of impotence, and as I began working with him, he experienced his head disconnected and floating above his body. As he began to reconnect his head to his body, his repressed sexual feelings toward his mother came up. Here his sexuality was so fused with his mother that he felt no sensation in the *head* of his penis, and the sensations were in his head (Ph.D. Chemist from Harvard). Reconnecting his head to his body somehow forced the sensations of sexuality for his mother to emerge.

Developmentally, disconnection helps a child survive. Disconnection means being over there, rather than here. Disconnection occurs when external reality is threatening. The child handled this and survived by *taking off*, checking out, or disconnecting. A child of an alcoholic or abusive family might *check out* to avoid the painful present. Often in cases of incest, a person might *check out* to avoid contact. Later in life, the disconnection remains as a trance, and intimacy cannot occur.

As mentioned earlier, the other side of disconnection is, classically, *fusion*.

4. Fusion

Fusion was an understanding developed in Structural Family Therapy by Salvador Minuchin and Braulio Montalvo, and in Strategic Family Therapy by Jay Maley and Cloé Madanes.

Fusion is a trance in which the *observer* creates a child identity in which a child over-identifies with and fuses with a family member. Sometimes this can occur when the child is asked to take care of a family member, commonly called *caretaking*. The child has to look after a dysfunctional parent in order to survive. The *observer* creates two parts of the child. One takes care of the dysfunctional parent and another fuses and becomes the dysfunctional parent.

An example is child abuse. In most cases, grown men and women who sexually abuse children were themselves abused as children. The *observer* during the abuse creates an image of a victimized child and an abuser. From this point on, the child within the adult has two parts; victim of the abuse, and the abuser. Fusing with the perpetrator is a key to working with incest survivors. As an adult, the abuser-part of the child within projects the child who was abused on other children, and abuses them. It is the dark side or abuser-part of the inner child (inside the adult) which feels the compulsion to abuse. The abuser child within is on automatic and out of control as an adult. This is the power of the dark side of the inner child.

Recently, a physician sent me a client he described as "spiritual." When I saw her, she complained of two problems: (1) she couldn't feel, and (2) the voices in her mind were telling her she was bad, evil. So, "I hate myself," she said.

At first, she gave me this very long story about how she left her body and floated to the top of the room. This part of her was her spirit. (See Chapter 14, Spiritualization). I asked her, "Were you ever physically or sexually abused?" She said, "Yes, my stepfather would beat me mercilessly while verbally abusing me." I said, "When did you start leaving your body?" She said, "During the beatings." I suggested that leaving the body automatically was a defense against feeling the pain of the beatings, and not "spiritual." She cried saying, "It is the only hope I have." I said, "It *was* the only hope you had, but it is now creating problems for you in present time."

This is an example of spiritualizing and disconnecting. The little girl disconnected from her body in order not to feel pain. But a part of her felt the pain and fused with the voice of her abusive stepfather, taking on his words and freezing them in her own head, resisting them and repeating them to herself over, and over, and over, yielding feelings of self-hatred. I wish to note she only saw me twice and it was not resolved in my office. I say this to emphasize that abuse is a serious issue and is not resolved by brief therapy. Severe abuse requires patience and knowledge on the part of the therapist, awareness and the ability to confront what occurred on the part of the client.

Structural and Strategic Family Therapy

In these two widely used forms of family therapy, the child often is brought to therapy with a problem, e.g., disobeying Dad/Mom, being disrespectful, drugs, teen pregnancy. In these models of therapy, the child might fuse with Mom who is angry with Dad, and the child becomes Mom's angry voice. The treatment is to separate the child from being the mother's spokesperson (de-fuse), and have the mother speak for herself to the father. In this case, the child believes she is helping or protecting Mom. Actually, the child is fusing with the parent, which diverts the parents' attention from handling their own relationship problems.

The depth of this trance, taking on someone else's identity to survive, can be seen in relationships. For example, many clients tell me that they sound like their mother when they yell at their kids or husband. Or, a husband will become just like his father in business. I had a client recently who claimed, "I am a workaholic." I said, "Are you a workaholic or did you *fuse* with your father who was a workaholic?" He said, "I fused with my father." The *child within* became Dad. The adult wants to spend time with his family. The child that fused with Dad's workaholism won't let him. This case was interesting because the father of my client was married to a woman who had several emotional breakdowns and was institutionalized. The father of my client became a workaholic to avoid seeing and dealing with his spouse. Not surprisingly, the child inside my client married a dysfunctional woman with severe emotional problems, and the other side of the child within became a workaholic—all outside of the *observer's* awareness. My client totally fused with and, like a xerox machine the *observer*, made a duplicate copy of Dad's trance.

This is another dark side of the inner child—taking on Dad's identity. I've had clients who are depressed. I'll ask, "Are you depressed, or did you take on your Mom/Dad's depression to help Mom/Dad?" An *observer* created a child identity which thinks they can help Mom or Dad by taking on their pain. The child takes on his parents' pain with the hope of healing them. This occurs when the child now believes they can heal others or make others feel better because of their imagined power. This infantile grandiosity leaves the child imagining power to help another, when they actually feel powerless as children. Years later, they develop a *healer* trance, imagining they can be responsible for taking away another's pain. For example, I once knew a man who claimed to be this kind of healer. Clients paid him to heal them and, amazingly, he, at times, got results. The problem was that the client's pain almost always came back. Why? Because, if a person is feeling pain, they must *take responsibility* for their subjective reality. When I spoke to the healer, he said that as a child he would *imagine* that being with his dysfunctional father helped his father feel better. In fact, his father would often times *lighten-up* around his son. Later in life the child within *imagined* magical powers as a way to resist the powerlessness of his childhood. Hence, the age-regressed child within hypnotized the adult into becoming a healer.

It needs to be noted that I am not discounting healers. I am, however, suggesting that for a healing to take place, the person being healed must be *conscious, aware,* and *responsible* for their internal experience. If they are not responsible, and not willing to make internal and external changes, the healing will be temporary and will not last. If someone thinks someone else can take their pain, they are in an inner-child identity and will probably be drawn to a healer who is, also, in an age-regressed inner-child identity imagining they can take another's pain.

In my life, my inner child always chose women who would argue with me. ("I want a girl, just like the girl who married dear old Dad"). After years of therapy and six years in a treatment facility (in India called an Ashram), I was aware of the problem and could interrupt the process. Still my inner child was working. One night, my best friend, David took me to watch Sufi Dancing in Los Angeles. About 75 people were there, some watchers, some doers. Before the dance started, I saw a woman enter and in a moment it was "Some enchanted evening, you may see a stranger..."

She asked David to introduce us, and this was the conversation.

David: "This is my friend Narayan (my name given in India), he's from ... India."

Woman:	"Oh, I just saw the film *Ghandi*. It was great."
Stephen:	"I didn't like it." (She looked confused, so to save the day I said,) "Well, for a long movie, it really moved fast."
Woman:	"Really? I thought it dragged."
Stephen:	"Well, I guess you and I aren't going to agree on anything."
Woman:	"I don't even agree with you on that."

Needless to say, I saw the pattern of my inner child, interrupted it, and this relationship lasted 10 seconds rather than 10 months or 10 years.

This is the power of *attraction* of the inner child. As an adult, you are attracted to certain people. Actually, the overwhelming, compulsive attraction is the inner child's attraction to another's inner child.

Very often, inner-child to inner-child connections are so strong that the child within the adult adapts a spiritual philosophy like, "This was meant to be," or "We are soul mates." Although this falls under the trance of spiritualization, dis-connection and other trances overlap and work in tandem.

As with all trances, fusion is created by a series of family interactions. For example, an individual may be an "adult child of an alcoholic" and had to take care of parents or siblings. They experienced not being able to let go, daydream, fantasize, or even play. Fear of possible catastrophic outcomes in the environment cause the child to be overly responsible (for the non-functioning parent). Thus, a hyper-vigilance trance.

I had a woman whose father was alcoholic and she always took care of him. Her philosophy was, "I'll take care of him, so that he can take care of me." She had to over-identify and watch every move Dad made so that she could survive. The child had to create a hyper-vigilant trance, watching Dad's every move, because he would space out, forget things, etc. The child within the adult stayed frozen in time and married a man who was very disconnected and spaced out. This was *famil*-(iar) to her inner child, whose dark side was attracted to men with whom she had to be hyper-vigilant, as with Dad. As a result, the child within the adult took over, never allowing her a moment's peace. Notice how her inner child had fused with Dad so the inner child had two sides: a spaced out side and a hyper-vigilant side. It is no wonder she was attracted to a disconnected man. It was familiar.

The inner child forced her to shrink her focus of attention and fuse with Dad and allowed her to be over-identified. This created serious anxiety as a child and in her life with her husband, particularly as the trance became more and more automatic. In other words, as the *observer* sleeps, the trance works by itself outside individual conscious control. It becomes an "automatic" trance.

Couples

Recently, I saw a couple for therapy in which the husband disconnected. He was out-there and disconnected and she over-identified. This problem emerges often in couples therapy. The complaint from the wife, "He's at work, he's doing this, he's doing that, I'm stuck with the kids. I'm here. He's there," He's disconnected from being here, and She's over-identified with being here, and she cannot disconnect and be there. During the therapy, I discovered the father of this woman was an alcoholic. She handled this in childhood by becoming the *caretaker*. She had to take care of the situation, always be there, or identify, take care of her father, her mother, the family. It was her job, so she identified and fused. She had to stay here, glued. If she didn't, who knew what would happen? She perceived her father might crack up the car; she had to feed the kids, be responsible, etc.

The *observer* handled the situation by creating an inner child identity which utilized the trance of over-identification. As I started doing therapy with her, she became terrified at the prospect of letting go. People who dis-connect, on the other hand are terrified if asked to be *here*. They will be frightened because as children they handled life by going away. It was too painful to deal with the reality of their family. My client experienced fear. If she went there, even for a minute, she heard a voice saying, "Where are you going? We need you to take care of Daddy." If the husband who disconnected stayed *here*, the experience was equally awful. The reality was bombarding and overwhelming for him.

Complementary Trances of the Inner Child

Often spouses have inner children who have trances that complement one another. In the former example, she over-identified and he disconnected.

We will explore complementary trance patterns of the inner children within the adult who pick familiar partners.

Oppositional Trances

Age Regression	Pseudo-orientation in Time *(Futurizing)*
Amnesia	Hypermnesia
Hyper-Sensitivity	Sensory Distortion (Numbing-out)
Dissociation (Disconnection)	Over-Identification (Fusion)
Hypnotic Dreaming	Over-identification
Negative Hallucination (Blocking-out)	Positive Hallucination Illusioning)

Wolinsky, *Trances People Live: Healing Approaches in Quantum Psychology., p. 113.*

It's clear that we all disconnect or over-identify in many different ways. It is important, in alcoholic cases particularly, for the symptom to be maintained; alcoholics have to disconnect and "go away." It can be said that alcohol and drug abuse is a way to use substances to disconnect. In order for the trance of drinking not to occur, de-hypnosis can be employed. Without the trance, the behavior has a more difficult time, automatically repeating itself outside your control.

The outward manifestation of alcoholism is drinking. Disconnection holds that problem like glue. If disconnection were not present, excessive drinking would be more difficult.

The question also arises, "Who drinks?" *The fused side of the inner child*, the child who fuses with the alcoholic Mom or Dad. I once had a client who handled stress with heavy drinking. I asked him, "Who drank in your family?" He said, "Dad." I had him carry around a picture of his father. Whenever he drank, he had to take out the picture, put it on the table and "toast" Dad saying, "Thank you, Dad, for teaching me how to handle stress." This exaggerated the inner child's fusion.

A symptom can only be a problem if there is some kind of trance. When a person is "being here now," there is no trance. Actually, we can say no problem can exist without a trance. This can be seen as the real meaning of the word transcending. In other words, trance ending a problem means *trance*-ending, when a trance ends and there is no problem you are in no trance. This is the end of trance, hence, *trance*-ending.

I know people that look directly at me but are not with me at all. There is a film over their eyes. Watch their eyes and notice if a film comes over them. Recognize this is a clue your partner is disconnecting. This film over his eyes indicates he is watching an old film or movie and not being here now. In therapy, I might suggest something to intentionally create the trance you are having. I PRESCRIBE THE CREATION OF THE TRANCE THAT CLIENTS ARE ALREADY CREATING. If someone has a film over her eyes, she is watching a movie inside which prevents her from experiencing *now*. Trances act like glue for problems. Signals, that a trance may be occurring in yourself, are holding your breath or tightening your muscles.

An example is a client who weighed 300 pounds. I identified an obesity problem (see how brilliant I am). In order for him to maintain his symptom, he disconnected. I suggested he go "over there," and his body froze hard (Sensory Distortion, Chapter 13). I suggested he make it get even harder to give him control over his trance. All of a sudden, he looked at me and said I was a "big cloud" to him. He could barely see me. This "not seeing" was a blocking-out trance, (See Chapter 8).

Disconnection occurs in people with migraine headaches or other types of physical pain. They have isolated specific physical pain to individual parts of their body. In order for a problem to be a problem, the headache must be disconnected from the *whole* body.

Complimentary Trances

I recently had a case of a woman whose father would lock her in a dry well. As a result, her body was still feeling pain years later. I understood experiencing the pain of 25 years ago was partly due to the inner child's trance of identification. Consequently, I taught her the deep trance of disconnection, its complement. Development of the complement of deep trance facilitates or *adds* water to the glue that holds the problem structure together, diluting the glue, and often times freeing the problem.

The Next Step
Handling Disconnection
and Over-identification

1. *Identify* which style of disconnecting the inner child is using.
   a. Not owning trance
   b. Disappearing trance
   c. I am not my body trance
   d. Fusion trance
2. Notice whether it occupies physical space, and/or mental space.
3. If your inner child is having you spacing out or disconnecting, create it fully, continuing to breathe. Intentionally tighten your muscles and create the disconnection. Tighten your muscles many times, until you have taken charge of the disconnected portion.
4. *Exaggerate*. For over-identification and dis-connecting, create the over-identification and muscle tightening. Just as above, the process will awaken the *observer*.
5. Notice that you are the *observer/creator* of one of the problem trances of the inner child.
6. Practice creating and stopping creating the trances of the inner child.

Summary

To identify and notice that the inner child is hypnotizing you in present time by disconnecting or over-identifying is the major solvent to dissolving the automatic processes of the inner child. Learning to live without trances, and that we are the *observer* and the creator of our subjective experience, dissolves trances of the inner child. This is the end of trance and is *trance*-ending.

•7

Inner Dialogue: The Voices in Your Head

Self-talk, or inner dialogue, is created by a series of interactions between the child and his or her parents. As with fusion, the *observer* takes the voices of both parents and places them in the inner child's head. In this way, a child takes the parents along inside of himself. As time goes by, the talk goes on as automatic chatter in the mind. Spend a minute noticing the voices telling you things inside your head, and notice if you can discern whose voices they are (mother, father, teacher, brother, sister, etc.). The dark side of the inner child limits the adult by continuing to talk to him or her self, often forecasting behavioral inevitabilities ("It will never work"), or suggesting what he or she should or shouldn't have done ("You shouldn't have said what you feel").

In cognitive therapy, "shoulds" are considered a thinking distortion.

"In this distortion, you operate from a list of inflexible rules of how you and others *should* act. The rules are right and indisputable. Any deviation from your particular values are *bad*. As a result, you are often in a position of judging and finding fault." (McKay, 1981:24)

In Gestalt therapy, "shoulds" are considered parental injunctions and are referred to as the "top dog." The child who "wants" is the underdog. In this situation, the child is in a double bind. If he does what he wants, the result is guilt, if he does what he *should* (the parental voice), he feels frustrated at not getting what he wants.

The key thing to note is that the inner child has fused with "should" voices that actually belong to the parents.

Handling the Shoulds

Step I: Notice that the should voice is occurring.

Step II: Notice where in the body the voice is coming from.

Step III: Notice *whose* voice it is, Mom, Dad, brother, sister, etc.

Step IV: *Intentionally* create the voice several times and experience the voice as energy.

Step V: Notice *you* are the *observer* observing the voices..

Inner Dialogues can be voices inside, consciously or unconsciously, that the inner child repeats to herself, creating problem states. In this case, they fuse the adult in the child trance. These are two sides of the inner child: (1) the child, and (2) the parent, both living inside the adult in present time.

A re-enforcement of the inner dialogue occurs within the family. In this system, the spouse or family can say or re-enforce the inner child's self-talk, thereby reinforcing her problems. For example, an inner child phrase, "What's wrong with me?" can be reinforced when the family or the spouse says, "What's wrong with you?"

Self-talk is not always verbal; it can be nonverbal, or silent. The individual can infer or intuit through silence or nonverbal cuing. As an example, a parent that is silent, never enquiring about the child's well being, might deliver the message, "Nobody is interested in you." Self-talk is always part of a problem and is implicit in many trance states.

Where does Self-Talk Come From?

An unprogrammed person, or a child before all the beliefs and ideas are suggested by the parents, is a pure *observer* or witness to life. The *observer* just observes; things happen or don't happen and the open blank slate of the observer is just present. The beauty of this *observer* is that there is no judgment, such as this is bad or that is good. Also, the child places no evaluations on things, such as this is better than that. Further, the *observer* places no significance on what it observes, such as, because this happens, it means this about me or about who I am.

The *observer* however, does begin to make creative decisions. First, this is *my* body, and that is *their* body. Later on, the parents begin to reward and punish, giving the child their judgements, evaluations, and significances about what life is, should be, could be, or what things mean. The *observer* becomes the creator and adapts by pushing the record button, tape-recording the parents voices, and taking a picture of a time frozen child who will hold onto these voices. For example, a parent may say to the child, "You should never trust people." The *observer/creator* takes a photocopy (picture) and creates a child within who records these voices. *Many of the voices we have in our heads about who or what we are, are the taped duplications of our parents' voices held within the frozen inner child.*

The *observer* has a blank audio tape with the record button on. The tape is filled up and has an auto-reverse, then the play button is pushed to hear the taped voices inside your head. These are the voices that the observer has recorded, they are being re-played by the child inside the adult. These voices can cause fear, anxiety or depression. But whose voices are these? The *observer* tapes the voices and they are played through the *speaker* of the inner child, then the voices of the parents are played again and again *automatically*. Years later, the inner child within the adult runs the machine. By creating the voices intentionally, the observer awakens to the voices *it (the observer)* has duplicated and thus takes back the power from the inner child. Once the *observer* is awakened and takes responsibility for making the tape and playing it through the inner child, the observer can turn off or stop creating the tape loop.

Inner dialogue is a trance that was created and allowed to persist. *Self-talk* was formed during a series of interactions (parents to child) and was designed by the parents to create an altered state of consciousness in the child. For example, a mother might suggest that her son or daughter be a certain way. The child then incorporates Mom's voice inside to remind himself how to be an adult, how to act. The suggestions were offered by the parents, siblings, etc., and were taped as truths. Problems arise when these voices are still talking, even though present circumstances do not fit the instructions given by the mother in past time.

Another illustration of *self-talk* is this: A child is told he doesn't understand how to operate the television. The child is offered suggestions by the parent, like "You don't understand," which the child decides to incorporate into his taped belief system. The child *generalizes* the belief about TVs to other mechanical devices, like cars, VCRs, computers. The *observer* creates an inner child which fuses with the suggestions made from the parent. He takes the suggestions on, as his own. Years later, the self-talk continues, and as the adult attempts to fix something, the inner child pushes the play button and a voice says, " I don't understand mechanical things."

The child within, when involved with mechanics, plays the taped message. The child within experiences the "I don't understand" associated with machines, along with frustration as its outcome or the altered state it produces. Machines trigger the experience, and the child as an adult goes into the "I don't understand" trance.

Principle I: An experience, once occurring following a pleasant outcome, will become part of the person's belief system exactly *as it is*.

As an example, a child is learning to read. Dad says, after the child struggles through it and succeeds, "See, if you work hard, you can do anything." The child has received his reward and approval and begins to "work hard" obsessively to do everything to get approval. Here, the hypnotic suggestion "work hard" can become frozen, an external trigger like money or approval, which then triggers "work hard and receive approval." This is placed on automatic. The resulting experience is one of feeling driven and yet experiencing it is never quite enough.

Another style of self-talk which overlaps is "fusion" and will only be discussed in brief.

An *observer* who creates a child identity which tries and fails at a task several times and hears Dad say, "This is how you do it," can "become" or fuse with the Dad and decide, "I'll be Daddy, and it will all work out." Of course, they begin to be so much like Daddy, they can lose themselves.

If the child resists Daddy, (rebellious boy), fusion takes place. The experience becomes "always fighting father."

This creates *Principle II*: When a fused identity is resisted, the resisting identity (rebellious boy) must be formed to protect the individual from the fused identity, namely Dad. "I must resist Dad" gets created. This appears as the *only* way an individual can survive.

Now you have two inner-child identities fighting one another. One is called "I'm like Dad," the other "I want to be me" (rebellious boy). This is experienced as an internal conflict. These two opposing inner-child identities keep the conflict in place.

Principle III: The resisting identity, when not in conflict with the fused identity, "Dad," will tend to *fight* the fused identity "Dad" outside themselves, whether present or imagined, and resist the imaginary Dad (fused identity).

This is clearly the trance of *trance*-ference. Transference, which is a major part of the psychoanalytic model of Sigmund Freud, briefly states that the client projects the parent on the therapist and then treats the therapist like Mom or Dad.

In this example, the rebel side of the inner child *trance*-fers Mom/Dad on to an authority figure, whether it is there or not, and begins to resist the authority figure. The difference is, in this model, the adult does not transfer or project Mom and Dad onto an authority figure; it is the *inner child* who is the culprit, *trance*-ferring images of Mommy and Daddy on people and acting like a little kid expecting to be taken care of. Transference is a trance of the inner child because the child goes into a trance and transfers Mom and Dad on others. This makes present time into past time, hence, *trance*-ference. For de-hypnosis to occur the *observer*, who has been asleep, must *wake-up* and take responsibility for this internal conflict.

As an example, the rebel (resisting Dad) identity called "I want to be me," will imagine, experience, or expect someone in authority to give her a hard time. It appears as though the person is attempting to be herself, while the inner child is actually reacting to a transferred image of Mom or Dad. Stated another way, the fused Father is projected or *trance*-ferred. The rebel (I want to be me) identity stays inside or vice versa. This explains why many people automatically assume that authority figures will push them around and they begin to fight them *before* that actually occurs.

How does this apply to self-talk? The child becomes the Father by duplicating the father's voice through a series of interactions with Father; the child identifies and fuses, through verbal dialogue, or non-verbal body posture, his looks, expressions, feelings and even tapes of the father's voice. If the child chooses to resist his father, he reflects a rebel identity. The rebel identity only creates and gives self-talk to itself in reaction to the father, which is now internalized. Thus, the inner and outer dialogue keep going. The inner child has two parts, rebel and Dad. If he is the rebel, he trance-fers Dad on others; if he is Dad, he projects the rebel on others.

The Next Step
Handling Inner Dialogue Trances

Step I: Notice your self-talk exactly, and write it down:

Examples:

>   Don't trust people.
>   Don't be close.
>   Don't touch me.

Step II: Ask whose voices these are?

    a. Mom
    b. Dad
    c. Uncle
    d. Aunt
    e. Teacher
    f. Brother
    g. Sister
    h. Grandparent, etc.

Step III:

    a. Intentionally create the voices.
    b. Next, move the voices into the left ear.
    c. Move the voices into the right ear.

Step IV: Notice if there are any feelings associated with a voice. Write them down.

Step V: Practice turning the voices (tapes) on and off, until you get mastery over the taped voices.

Step VI: Observe each voice, and notice that you, as the observer, exist with or without the voices.

This is important to note, because often the only way a child can exist as a separate individual is to resist Mom or Dad. This rebel or outsider identity gets formed. This is difficult to give up because the person imagines that without the rebel or outsider, he would not exist, be annihilated, or disappear. Once the observer is established, letting go of old identities becomes easier. This is because there is a *you* beyond the rebel or outsider with whom you can identify.

Conclusion

It cannot be over emphasized, in either working with yourself or working with another, that inner dialogue needs to be identified and handled. Inner dialogue is the cornerstone of reality formations and affective states. Within fusion, or reaction to fusion, unless the individual has a choice of internal messages or dialogue, he can never experience freedom from prior family trances, especially the trance of trance-ference. Furthermore, although the *observer* made the tapes of mom or dad, they are now playing *through* the age-regressed inner child. The *observer* is asleep and takes no responsibility for this. By developing observation, the *observer* wakes-up, and the trance of the inner-dialogue is *trance*-ended.

•8

Blocking-out: Not Seeing What Is There

Blocking-out is a trance state that consists of not seeing what is there (visual), and/or not hearing what is said (auditory). As with all trances, blocking-out is developed by the *observer* to protect, support, and maintain the child's survival, and to preserve his integrity as an *individual self.*

The blocking-out phenomenon becomes a problem as this trance of the inner child becomes more and more independent, operating autonomously while the *observer* sleeps. The inner child continues not to see, by fogging-out or blanking-out what is there. This worked in the family context and continues on automatic, even in present time situations where it is not called for.

For example, imagine a little girl who had to fog out when her father sexually assaulted or battered her mother. Years later, even though the context has changed, she fogs out appropriate requests for intimacy from a safe partner or repeatedly chooses a partner who is a batterer. What must be understood is that, although the fogging out helped the child survive, it did not work 100%. Some part of the child saw the assault. This creates an inner child with two sides, side one fogs out, and side two sees the assault. The time frozen-inner child automatically re-creates the trance that worked in the past, not seeing. Carrying it over into present time, the adult is simultaneously attracted to a famil-(iar) scene, battering. In the former case, even though the adult wants to make contact, the inner child keeps blocking-out. Ideally, blocking-out should be like a sun screen. If I go to the beach and am able to *choose* the degree of exposure I want by picking the right level of sun screen, I am at *choice*. But, if I can't get the protection I want, I am at the mercy of the sun, or the dark side of an out-of-control, wounded inner child.

It should be noted again, that women who choose men that batter either saw Mom being battered or were battered, themselves. Thus the trance of blocking-out is not a solution. The child within is attracted to the familiar scene, even though the adult knows better; and the *observer* sleeps.

Interpretive Distortion

One example of kinesthetic blocking-out, (See Chapter 13, Sensory Distortion) can occur in an interpretive experience. For example, in cases of child abuse the child might at first experience the abuse painfully. As the experience is repeated again and again, the child might begin to interpret physical or emotional abuse as pleasurable, affectionate or loving. Interpretative distortion constitutes a subtle form of kinesthetic blocking-out, not feeling what is there. This interpretation explains an individual's addictions to emotionally and physically abusive relationships. It is no surprise that children who were sexually abused either abuse others or get abused as adults. The child within assumes that forced sex and abuse are love, affection, or worse yet, the "way it is."

I had a client who, for several years of her marriage, was raped by her husband. Her gynecologist asked her if she had been raped, because there was so much vaginal tearing. Although she didn't enjoy the experience, she interpreted it as "*the way it is.*"

In transactional analysis negative strokes are considered better than no strokes. This is a particularly difficult process in that the blocking-out is interpreted as enjoyable or as how it should be, and is therefore not questioned, nor acknowledged.

I saw a man once whose father was a minister in Southern Ohio. His father quite often would bring the boy down to the basement. There he would have him pull down his pants, and spank him. The boy felt incredible pain, but eventually interpreted the sensations as pleasurable. Years later, he was involved in sado-masochist sex. Upon entering therapy, he felt that his interest in being physically hurt, which gave him sexual pleasure, was going too far, i.e., he had put himself in life-threatening situations. After many sessions, images began to appear in his memory. While his father was spanking him, his father would masturbate. Here the child within blocked out the pain of the spanking and interpreted it as pleasurable, because it was the only way he seemed to get love and affection from Dad. Years later, this generalized to the only way to get sexual love and affection: by being spanked or hurt physically.

Blocking-out occurs when the development or survival of the child is dependent upon *not* seeing, hearing, feeling or even knowing (see Chapter 12, Amnesia) what is occurring. Blocking-out is created by the child in the family context by a series of interactions as the child develops. Blocking-out can be continued by the family and later the spouse. For example, an alcoholic man who abuses his wife might suggest she block out his drinking or abuse. This could be a continuation of the suggestions of her parents that saved her as a child, "Don't see the drinking."

Often times, the *observer* models the inner child within her mother, and creates a duplicate inner child within the adult, not seeing her father drinking. This child assumes that's how one handles drinking, the way mom modeled; *by blocking-out*. The child models Mom's trance. It is no wonder that as an adult she will not see her husband drinking and might even enable him to drink more. Often in therapy I ask clients, "Who was the model for that trance?", or "Who demonstrated this technique of survival? i.e., blocking-out." Stated more simply the blocking-out phenomenon can be put on automatic and pops up, has its own life. It is a once valuable trance created by the child for survival, or imitated by the observer by modeling the parent, and carried into adult life. This limits other possible experiences and creates unpleasant behavioral outcomes. The old habit of blocking-out is so powerful that the individual cannot understand his confusion and pain, which come from interpersonal relationships in present time.

How people construct their reality is central in understanding blocking-out. By creating the fog, cloud, a feeling of distance, the problem is maintained. Why? Because the blocking-out strategy is not 100% effective. Some part of the child sees the abuse and chooses people to re-create the abuse, so the other side of the child can block it out! Questions to ask yourself are, "By not seeing what is there, how do I deny the problem? How do I participate in picking abusive relationships? What trance(s) is connected with or associated with my particular problem?"

Every addictive person I've worked with uses blocking-out. In order for their symptom to remain, they have to fog-out the world as they did as children. This symptom can emerge as an auditory blocking-out, a visual blocking-out, a kinesthetic blocking-out (sensory distortion), or a not knowing blocking-out (amnesia/denial). The important element is recognizing you do NOT see, know, feel, or hear what's occurring. In cases of drug and alcohol abuse, the substance helps to intensify the blocking-out. In other words, the psychological ability to block out is not strong enough. Therefore, drugs must be employed.

For example, if a client says, "I know you're judging me," his inner child is both blocking-out and catastrophizing. They are not seeing *me* in present time. If I say, "You look good today," the client can block hearing the good things. Notice if blocking-out helps you to avoid particular experiences, either by blocking parts of yourself or by blocking-out the world.

I treated an alcoholic woman who would block out as a child, in her family setting, in order to survive. Later in life, she continued blocking, which affected her relationships. This is no surprise. Blocking was her trance of choice, or her drug of choice. Her drinking problem had to contain elements of this phenomenon. The only way she could drink was to not see the world.

As mentioned earlier, one side of the inner child blocked out the father's drinking, while the other side saw the drinking. She naturally will pick a relationship where either she fogs out the person's drinking or, she drinks and the other person fogs out her drinking. Notice how the inner children of both people have complimentary trances. For therapists what is noteworthy is that, as you approach the drinking side of the inner child, the fog gets thicker. Why? Because the two work together, the fog and the drinking must be looked at as one function of the inner child.

Blocking-out Your Body

There is a form of blocking-out that is similar to retroflection. This phenomenon can best be understood by a case example. Recently I was working with a woman who was an incest survivor. The pain was so intense that she tried to block out her father. This was ineffective, so she retroflected the block on herself. Simply stated, she attempted to fog out her father, and when that did not work, she fogged out herself in an attempt to become invisible. When she came to me in therapy, she told me that when she looked in the mirror, she could not see her body. It was fogged out! I have seen this in many cases of child abuse where there is an attempt to be invisible and fog out one's body. The child cannot make the perpetrator invisible, so he freezes himself, making his body invisible.

Therapeutic Approach

My strategy is to ask clients to look at me, which interrupts their child trance and starts a present time experience. As they look at me, they don't feel lonely. There is no blocking-out occurring with me. If she is connecting with me, and really connects, how could she experience loneliness? In present time, we are just here. If she blocks me out and goes into her child trance, she experiences loneliness because she is her inner child, which is not in present time but in past time. Stated more simply, you will feel lonely if you are operating out of an inner-child identity trance, because you are not in present time seeing, hearing, feeling, knowing and being. The inner child cuts off present-time contact and feels the loneliness of no contact in past time.

Principle IV: In order for the inner child to shift from a present time experience of self to a past time experience, the inner child must cut off present time contact, hence loneliness, alienation, feeling misunderstood, etc.

In the earlier example, the sexually abused woman is blocking-out in her relationships. When she makes love with a man, she opens her eyes and blocks the man out. She does not see this man, who states, "I want to be your friend and an occasional lover." He is being very clear about what he wants. She is blocking-out his communication visually and auditorially. She fantasizes, "No, he can't be saying that, he really means ...."

Notice how blocking-out and fantasizing work so well in tandem. In the above scenario, "I know he means something else," she experiences no variability in her trance; rather, the inner child's trance, created by the observer, keeps the present-time adult stuck.

The Next Step
Handling Blocking-out

Approach I:

1. *Identify.*

The basic principle is to identify and allow the blocking-out to be there fully. This means to literally invite the phenomenon to reach its full fruition. In other words, if you're fogging out, don't push through or resist the fog. Rather breathe, and allow the fog to manifest. See the fog completely, its size, shape, color, etc.

2. *Expand.*

Expand the experience of the fog, clouding, blanking, by making it bigger.

3. *Differences.*

Make it different, by moving it around, change its color, shape, size, smell or feeling.

4. *Differentiating.*

Vary its structure. As a general rule, by varying the components of the trance, it is possible to take charge of its coming and going. This takeover by the observer/creator removes the trance from an automatic response to a conscious, self-generated response. In differentiation, notice color, transparency, translucency, and opaqueness. This causes the trance to shift from being one solid mass to a varied experience, with different integrity levels.

Approach II:

Answer these questions on a separate piece of paper. Keep asking the questions, writing down whatever pops up, until nothing else pops up.

1. Where is the inner child in your body?
2. Ask the inner child, "What am I willing to see?" Write down the inner child's answers.
3. Ask the inner child, "What are you (the inner child) unwilling to see?" Write down the inner child's response.
4. Ask the inner child, "What are you willing to hear?" Write down the inner child's answers.
5. Ask the inner child, "What are you unwilling to hear?" Write down the inner child's responses.

Approach III:

1. Ask the inner child, "What did you (the inner child) decide to see? Write down the inner child's answers.
2. Ask the inner child, "What did you (the inner child) decide to not see?" Write down the inner child's answers.
3. Ask the inner child, "What did you (the inner child) decide to hear?" Write down the inner child's answers.
4. Ask the inner child, "What did you (the inner child) decide to not hear?" Write down the inner child's answers.

Observe:

1. *Observe* that you are the witness of the inner child and his/her trances.
2. Continue to watch the inner child, adding awareness to the process.

3. Notice how observing adds the solvent of awareness to the inner-child identity. This process creates space or distance between you, the *observer* of the inner child, and his/her trance.

Conclusion

Blocking-out is a subtle and often unnoticed trance. Once noticed, the *observer wakes-up*, interpersonal communications alters, and an individual can see, feel, hear, know and be who he is in the present. Awareness and observation are the major tools used to take apart the inner child's I-dentity and his/her trances.

•9

Illusioning: Seeing, Hearing and Feeling What Is Not There

I was trying to catch your eye,
I thought that you were trying to hide
I was swallowing my pain
I was swallowing my pain

"Jealous Boy" John Lennon

Here John Lennon describes his illusioning. The inner child imagines his wife is trying to hide; and that she doesn't love him anymore. He age regresses and feels pain. In other words his illusioning of Yoko trying to hide, created a painful trance for the adult in present time.

Illusion: a false mental image or conception which may be a mis-interpretation of a real appearance or may be something imagined. (American College Dictionary, pg 602)

Selective Trances

The inner child sees past time, imagining it is present time, thus "illusions," seeing things now that were there then. In this way, the inner child within the adult reads into things now, things that were said then, feels things now that were felt then, but are not actually happening now, or hears things now that were said then. This dark side of the frozen inner child sets up internal, subjective experiences, some of which are based on present time information, but some of which are just free floating illusions from the past, that confuse, interfere with, and misinterpret present time reality.

In selective trances, the child within selects what was, or occurred in the past, and overlays it on the present or future. For example, a child whose father was dysfunctional is told by his mother (the hypnotist) how much Dad cares because he remembered a birthday, rather than acknowledging that Dad's been drinking every day this month and just happened to do *one* nice thing. Years later, the child within the adult marries an alcoholic and selects the one nice event and magnifies it. This selective trance mirrors the earlier trance suggested by Mom.

In illusioning, what is seen is not there, or more commonly, what is there is magnified as if it were the whole picture. It is similar to its complement, blocking-out, in that both trances require a shrinking of the focus of attention. In the above case, Mom is accentuating the positive (the remembered birthday) and pretending that that is all or most of reality.

Here we see the joint use of illusioning (selective seeing) and blocking-out (ignoring what is there). Many therapists suggest that the solution lies in focusing on the positive, by asking questions like, "What does he/she do that works for you?" The problem is that often the whole is ignored in favor of a small part in the hope that illusioning will promote a cure. The therapist, while in this mode of thinking, shrinks his focus of attention to see what works, and tries to accentuate the positive. The therapist asks the client to go into the

same trance the therapist is using in order to feel productive. Often, this form of therapy attracts a practitioner with a selective inner-child trance. The client and therapist go into a mutual trance.
In cognitive therapy this is called "filtering."

"This distortion is characterized by a sort of tunnel vision—looking at only one element of a situation to the exclusion of everything else."

"Each of us has our own particular tunnel to look through. Some of us are hyper-sensitive to anything suggesting loss, and blind to any indication of gain." (Mckay, 1981:19)

Wonderfulizing or Awfulizing

Wonderfulizing relates to the former example, in which Mom selected Dad's remembrance of the child's birthday to the exclusion of the daily drinking. Awfulizing is explained this way.

"By the very process of filtering you magnify and awfulize your thoughts. When you pull negative thoughts out of context ... you make them larger and more awful than they are." (McKay, 1981:19)

For example, a woman I was working with was molested by her uncle. During the process, her inner child stayed focused on his left eye. Years later, the time-frozen inner child would project and illusion the man she was with as her uncle by looking at his left eye. Awfulizing is a thinking distortion under the heading of illusioning or hallucination in trance land, or filtering in cognitive therapy land. (See Appendix, Trigger).

As with all trance states, an illusion was created by the observer to help protect the child from the strains of family interactions. Illusions that initially had a specific, external trigger (like the uncle), become problems as the trance is generalized to *all* men. This process is stimulated by the inner child focusing on the trigger, the left eye.

Another example is the woman who was molested as a child. The adult goes into a "don't trust" trance, even in an environment that is pleasant. Illusioning also is witnessed within families or couples that co-create survival illusions together, keeping the family together.

For example, a dysfunctional family might continually illusion themselves as fine, upstanding citizens and present themselves to the community that way. In many cases of incest or child abuse, the family creates this world view with a "Father Knows Best" illusion. In this television show, Jim was the perfect dad, little Kathy was a good girl, and Bud was a mischievous son. In real life, however, Jim was alcoholic and had several failed attempts at suicide. Kathy was sexually abused, and Bud had a drug addiction problem. Unfortunately, family members are asked to block out the uncomfortable and opt for the illusion of the positive image. This concept of the power of thoughts or the power of positive thinking will be discussed in Chapter 14, Spiritualization.

To form illusions, the child must shrink her focus of attention to a very small part of total reality, which part becomes magnified and greatly distorted. The remedy for seeing what is not there, is seeing what *is* there.

Illusioning, Futurizing, Fantasizing

Often, trances work together to create an illusion. A woman client reported she had been talking with "beings," guides that came to see her. They told her of events in the future, and that she was a chosen person. People would admire her and were waiting for her to become almost like Christ. She was further informed that she would have thousands of followers. These were very strong illusions. The problem at this point was she felt very anxious, because she was not ready to become like Christ. The client was reluctant to tell anyone of these illusions for fear she would be thought crazy. As we talked of these beings or guides, she became very young, and I could see in front of me the little girl inside the grown woman. The adult had become the age-regressed inner child. The *observer* had created this illusioning as a child because her home life had been intolerable. This is how she protected herself. In other examples of illusioning, people imagine a Cinderella story in which some millionaire will marry them and take them away from all this, take care of them, give them everything they need, give them undying love, attention, etc. People also envision being President, a baseball star, football hero, or a movie star. This ability to create illusions is how children remove themselves and disperse the reality of family experiences.

Case 1 explained: The client who created the illusion of being like Christ did so to help her survive as a child. The child's illusion might have simply ended. She might have switched to an illusion of herself as a school teacher. But these patterns of illusioning and futurizing often escalate, making the illusions solid. Hence, as an adult, the child within the woman experiences beings or guides coming to her. She is unable to sleep at night. She is waiting for the prophecies to come true. The illusions developed in childhood had become very strong.

Erickson's story of a man in a mental institution who thinks he is Jesus and sits waiting for his disciples also demonstrates this solidifying of illusions. The man/Jesus was so convinced that no therapists could talk him out of the trance. The story has it that Erickson *utilized* his trance to make a shift in his behavior. Erickson allegedly went over to the man and said, "I hear you are a carpenter." The Jesus/man is now in a double bind. If he says "no," then he's not Jesus. If he says "yes," then he doesn't know what will happen. He said "yes". Erickson said, "Come with me. There is some carpentry work that needs to be done in the new wing of the hospital." I don't know the conclusion to this story, but many of Erickson's stories seem to end with Erickson's illusion of health; and *"He got married and had three children."*

In the development of illusions, the greater the stress in life the stronger the illusions. Illusions can be sensory, auditory, or visual: seeing something that is not said, or hearing something that is not there, or feeling something that is not there.

Case 2: Upon my return from India, I was looking for an office in Albuquerque. One week before I arrived, a therapist had rented space from my doctor friend who owned a building. When I met the therapist who was renting the office, he looked uncomfortable learning I was a therapist looking for an office. He told my secretary, "His energy is *so* aggressive I can just feel it." Another doctor in the office said, "Wow, you feel great; I heard you just got back from

India; maybe we could meditate together some time." Who was feeling things that weren't there? I don't know, but certainly each inner child illusioned a different experience of "my energy." The therapist felt threatened and, hence, "my energy" was aggressive, the doctor wanted a friend to meditate with so, "my energy" felt great. The inner child can illusion and project it on a situation or person, and subjectively make it feel as though it is true. Each inner child determined his experience of my energy through his own needs. This is a form of illusioning, feeling what is not there, seeing and defining things as we need them to be seen and defined. My first teacher was the noted industrial psychologist Dr. Frederick Herzberg. Herzberg would sum it up this way, "We define things the way we need them to be defined."

Remedy of illusioning: Check it out with the other person. A reality check to see where the other person is coming from helps to determine if you are illusioning. This requires, however, a willingness to take responsibility for your *trance*-ferred feelings. It also requires you to look at yourself, rather than at another, as the creator of your experience.

A goal in therapy is to understand that the child within is illusioning. Look at it developmentally. In the case where the woman was to become Christ, the illusion of the child within began as the adult described her illusions. She began to look young, three or four years old. She was already in her age-regressed-child trance. The only way the small child could handle the bombardment she had to deal with was for the *observer* to develop a trance called illusioning, futurizing, and fantasizing. The child said, "Someday, it's going to be better."

A similar example might be a young boy who wanted to be a professional football player, but by the time he was 13, had given it up because of feedback from the world, i.e. he didn't make the team. He then wanted to be a basketball player. Since he was too short, he gave that up. He accepted feedback in present time a connection to the world, and integrated. When a person is in present time, he can allow and integrate feedback from the world. The individual will let go of illusions.

Lack of *feedback* solidifies illusions. When the child cuts off feedback (family or world) to survive, illusions become more solid and the intensity of the need not to see the family situation increases. Children often imagine stardom, but if they stay connected to the world in present time, they know when they can't play the guitar (feedback), and can't be Eric Clapton. In more severe cases, there is no feedback loop. Instead, the child goes into a child-to-child trance, cut off from present-time feedback (can't play guitar), and, years later, feels pain.

> **Principle V:** An *observer* relating to the world makes trances *trans*-ient and part of growing up. If the child does not shift to the feedback from the world because of the horror of a dysfunctional family, the child shifts to a child-to-child trance. Years later the child within hypnotizes the adult. This creates the adult's illusions.

Many people have illusions about being a movie or rock and roll star. This seems to be quite common. This is a way the child resists experiences in the family that are too painful to integrate at the time. Problems arise when the illusions become solid, and interpersonal feedback is cut off. For example, I wanted to play basketball for the Boston Celtics. By 13, I realized that I was going to be too small. I then illusioned being a coach. Soon I saw that I didn't have those skills and moved on to find where my skills were. This is a developmental process. If I had become obsessed with playing with Larry Bird and couldn't even give it up when I wasn't drafted, I might have experienced depression.

In the woman-who-was-Christ example, I asked the client to imagine that the guides who came to see her and the voices she heard were actually coming from the child inside her. I asked, "How would you feel if this is true?" She said, "Whew, relieved." She comfortably saw the illusions were coming from inside of her. She felt relieved. No anxiety. The important idea to note is that trances are a *continuum* from solid to liquid. We all use trances. Her trance wasn't bad, just more solid than mine. In my case I let go of the desire to be a basketball hero, integrating interpersonal feedback. In contrast, her developmental illusions solidified because she cut off interpersonal feedback.

I saw a film in the early 70s directed by Roman Polansky called *Repulsion,* which demonstrates illusioning. Part of the film is shot from the viewpoint of a young girl who is supposed to be a "paranoid schizophrenic." In one scene, her older sister is making sandwiches for them. The kitchen looks about 10 feet by 10 feet. When you see the room through the paranoid schizophrenic woman's eyes, it looks about 6 feet high by 4 feet, almost like a box. Next, there is a fly in the room as seen through the older sister's eyes. When the younger sister comes in, through her eyes, the room is crawling with insects. The question, of course, is "Who is illusioning?" By societal agreement the younger sister is. In reality, they both may be illusioning.

Case 3: A woman who had been sexually molested was illusioning snakes. She saw snakes pouring out of her mouth, her ears, and her vagina. Her inner child was illusioning in present time, the penis intrusions of past time. In other words, she shifted the penis intrusion to snakes to avoid the even greater pain of incest. Here is a continuum of illusioning in the way the child disperses the energy of child abuse. People illusion having a relationship with this person or doing that activity, or illusion themselves swimming the English Channel. The key is being able to recognize them as illusions. The inner child sometimes has to do something to maintain his integrity of self. One client could not see me (blocking-out) to the point where he could just see my lips and hear my voice. In this manner, I at least maintained contact with him. The illusioning phenomenon occurs in degrees and is a continuum.

Complementary Trances

Illusioning and blocking-out may occur simultaneously. Someone might be hearing something that is not there, and blocking-out what is there. This phenomenon happens in relationships. For example, imagine a man and woman are getting together for the first time and the man says, "You look nice." The woman hears, "He wants to sleep with me." The woman says, "I'd like to have lunch with you" and the man hears, "She really wants to have a relationship with me." That is the illusioning-blocking-out process.

In the Woody Allen film, *Annie Hall*, two characters have a conversation on the balcony. The conversation is about philosophy. Subtitles are added to the film, telling you what is being said behind the words. In illusioning, however, the subtitles are seen, even when they are not present. The child within *mind reads* them and acts *as if* they were there and real in present time.

Mind Reading

"When you mind read you make snap judgements about others... There's no evidence but it just seems right. In most instances, mind readers make assumptions about how other people are feeling and what motivates them... As a mind reader, you also make assumptions about how people are reacting to things around them, particularly how they are reacting to you.... Mind reading depends on a process of projection. You imagine that people feel the same way you do and react to things the same way you do. Therefore you don't watch or listen closely enough to notice that they are actually different." (Mckay, 1981:20)

For example, a sexually-abusive father might talk about the Boy Scouts with his son, but the child knows his father wants sex. The child is seeing the actual subtitles. The child within the adult, years later, sees subtitles with most men and feels scared. This is illusioning, taking the past subtitles and projecting them into the present.

With the illusioning of mind reading, the child within illusions what is occurring. Breaking the child-to-child loop so the observer can wake-up the inner child's trance and see present time, forces the causes of the mind reading to surface, which is scary.

Principle VI: The child-to-child trance must be maintained; the child-to-child trance must make the world conform to its image. To see the world otherwise would break the trance and bring about CHAOS.

Recently, I was giving a workshop in Quantum Psychology on the East Coast. A therapist came who was trained in N.L.P. (Neuro Linguistic Programming) and said this is just like N.L.P. I said well, there is no reframing, no parts negotiation, no swish technique, no modeling, no phobia model, no resource retrieval, no rapport building, and no anchoring, and no use of representational systems. She said, "It's just like N.L.P." I got confused until I realized she was in a child-to-child trance, trying to make me be her image rather than experiencing the *chaos* that might be evoked by new information. Somehow, the child within feels her world being threatened as the walls of the inner child are pierced with new information. Why? Because allowing new information in or present time feedback, breaks the trance of the inner child and awakens the observer. This causes the trauma to surface that caused the trance to be constructed in the first place. This could explain the almost violent reactions people have to new data.

In illusioning, the person is seeing what is not occurring. If they are blocking-out, they are not really seeing what is going on. A woman came to see me for counseling complaining that she always heard her mother's voice inside herself (inner child's auditory illusioning). I suggested she spend 20 minutes each evening imagining a record of her mother's voice playing at 45 rpms. I called it "Mom's Greatest Hits." She then was asked to regulate the speed from 45 rpms to 78 rpms to 33 rpms. She was further instructed to alternate the sound in each stereo speaker (ear). She could regulate the balance, also the treble, and bass. By doing this task for one week, she was able to awaken the *observer* and gain control over the voices which had popped up automatically.

The Next Step
Handling Illusioning

1. *Recognize.*

   Acknowledge the illusioning as the inner child.

2. Identify which style of illusioning is occurring.

   a. Selective trancing
   b. Awfulizing
   c. Wonderfulizing
   d. Mind-reading

3. *Call out.*

   Each time the illusioning occurs, internally call out its

name. For example, if you find the inner child is making everything awful (awfulizing), internally call out that process by name, pointing internally to it. Say to yourself, that's *awfulizing*.

4. *Vary.*

Create the illusions in a variety of ways, more, better, or different. By continually creating the illusioning in different ways, you gain control and cease creating the illusion.

5. *Moving.*

Another way of dismantling illusioning is to move the images around, to see them smaller, bigger and then in different parts of the room. This enables the person to take charge of the created image.

6. *Voice Control.*

For auditory illusionings, like hearing parental voices, the following techniques are helpful. Imagine a stereo with three speeds, 78, 33-1/3, and 45. Imagine the voice as if it were on the record. Play the voices fast, then medium, then slow. Make the sound louder, softer, and then shift the speakers. This is a way of taking charge of the audio illusioning.

7. Trance-ference.

If you notice you are projecting on men or women, imagine them as Mom or Dad. Intentionally create a mom and dad mask on *all* men and *all* women for a week. This will awaken the observer of the inner child, so the observer can take charge of the process.

Conclusion

Illusioning is a trance that can be appreciated for what it is—the inner child's defense. With this understanding, the adult can explore his inner child's defenses as "creative choices," and thus the observer can take charge of the automatic illusioning. This is respecting and appreciating the inner child's defenses as early solutions to *prior* problems, which have been dominating the subjective experience of present time. Furthermore, it cannot be overstated that waking up can be a painful process. Why? Because the *observer* created the trances to *dull* the pain of trauma. To awaken the *observer*, the pain of the trauma can no longer be denied or dulled. Hence, in the waking-up of the *observer* the trances must be acknowledged along with the denied trauma. It is only in that way that the awake *observer* can become an established state; or better said, an established non-state of *trance*-endence.

•10

Con-fusion:
Getting Lost

In Spanish, the word "con" means "with," so we might say that *with* fusion comes *con*fusion.

Confusion is the trance the *observer* creates and that occurs when the interaction in the family cannot be understood or integrated by the child. This happens when the *observer* and child are faced with an event, situation, or emotion that cannot be fully experienced. The child either resists experiencing the episode or he has no model to explain its occurrence. It is in this process that the experience of con-fusion emerges. For example, a child with parents who are mean to each other might experience con-fusion. This situation does not make sense to the child, and so the *observer* creates a confusion trance. A problem occurs when years later, the child within the adult automatically gets confused when there is an argument.

Confusion and Chaos

Recently, the emergence of the theory of chaos in physics has turned the world of science around. My forthcoming book interfaces principles of chaos with psychology and Eastern philosophy, and is called *The Tao of Chaos: Essence and the Enneagram, Quantum Consciousness, Volume II*. Trances are a way of organizing chaos. For example, a child being molested goes through a period of chaos, and to organize and handle that chaos, the observer develops strategies, identities, and trances to explain or cope with chaos.

Webster's definitions of chaos are, (1) utter confusion or disorder; wholly without organization or order. (2) The infinity of space or formless matter supposed to have preceded the existence of the ordered universe. (Webster's Dictionary, pg. 201)

Chaos for the purposes of this book includes states of confusion, being overwhelmed, out of control, feeling crazy, and emptiness or void.

In the resistance to the feeling of chaos comes the organization of trances, which hopes to make sense out of that which doesn't make sense or *does not compute*. Interestingly enough, Buddhists for centuries have said the greatest resistance people have is to emptiness (chaos).

Once an experience like being molested is resisted, the child will protect herself from experiencing the pain of knowing what happened, by surrounding it with confusion, and often several other trances. Often people will develop a spiritual philosophy to justify how they have organized the chaos, (See Chapter 14, Spiritualization).

Principle VII: It is a "shift" of consciousness from just observing the situation through confusion or chaos to creating identities to meet the unknown situation.

For example, a child who is asked to do something by Mom gets confused and, through trial and error, behaves the way Mom wants. Once re-enforced by Mom, situations that appear similar to the child create con-fusion and the inner child creates the same reaction (trance or identity) that worked before with Mom.

Simply put a child who eats with his hands receives a *not okay* look from Mom. If the *observer* cannot integrate the mother's message, confusion is created. In that shift of awareness from observing Mom and her message to creating a reaction that gets Mom's approval, coping devices emerge which can be called identities. In this situation one particular identity that might manifest is "I want to do it my way." With further intensification of the message by the mother, the *observer* again produces confusion and might create another identity called "Yes Mom, whatever you want." To make it even more interesting, the observer places the entire situation on automatic, goes to sleep and, thus, the inner child window to reality is born. He can now avoid thinking about new reactions in present time and can just keep creating the same old identity that worked with Mom. These two identities are now in opposition to one another. One identity says, "I want to do it my way," and the second identity, "I have to do it Mom's way to survive." Here again are two sides of the inner child. And as they generalize into other areas of life, they both create conflicts inside the adult as well as with others.

For example, the inner child might project one identity on her boss and feel she has to *kiss ass* in order to survive, believing, "I can never do it my way." As a boss, the inner child might project the "I want to do it my way" on an employee and demand, "It's my way or your fired."

This example is a simplification of the identity process although I am sure we all can imagine ourselves in school, marriage, or at work with these automatic conflicts occurring, which are inherent in identity formation. Look at the double bind, or lose-lose set-up. The child sees only two possibilities: unloved or fired. If the pretend identity conforms to survive, the adult feels lost, alienated and misunderstood.

Unfortunately, in our society, which is the context in which we live, conforming and giving oneself up is the rule. The advent of the industrial revolution is when the whole popularization of psychology emerged. Society asks people to "play the game" and psychology, a child of the industrial revolution, comes up with ways to help the child fit in. It is the fitting-in process that is confusing. It asks people to give up themselves to survive. Unfortunately, society with its child-like psychology supports that process by rewarding those who know how to "play the game" (money, status, etc.), and punishing those who feel the pain of "selling themselves out." Noted industrial psychologist, Frederick Herzberg would say that problems arise with adults because we ask them to act like responsible adults—*but treat them as children.* Herzberg would say, if you want someone to act as an adult, you must give them an adult job and treat them as adults. Herzberg contended that the assembly line of mechanized society asks adults to act and work as children. This, according the Herzberg, isn't possible, and so assembly line workers act as children with high turnover rates and low productivity.

Three Types of Confusion

1. Task Confusion

Confusion can take three forms. In the first type, parents make demands that are not possible to achieve or are viewed as overwhelming by the child. These overwhelming parental expectations, which the child is unable to fulfill, create feelings of confusion and chaos. The confusion becomes the mechanism or way the child handles the event. For example, the parent expects the child to make a peanut butter and jelly sandwich by himself at age three. The *observer* creates confusion and the child feels overwhelmed and confused. The confusion gets *generalized* to everything they are asked to do. Even years later they become overwhelmed and confused when asked to perform certain tasks. The confused inner child remains frozen, generalizing confusion onto many situations, events, or arenas. The child within the adult feels constant pressure to perform or do the task perfectly. Overtones of being judged or feelings of incompetency or inadequacy follow this trance. Confusion is placed on automatic by the *observer*, the *observer* goes to sleep and the inner child within the individual takes over and then fuses or associates confusion with tasks.

2. Over-generalization

In this thinking distortion you make a broad generalized conclusion based on a single incident or piece of evidence.... A rejection on the dance floor means, "Nobody will ever want to dance with me.... You are over-generalizing when you absolutely conclude that, "*Nobody* loves me, I'll *never* be able to trust anybody. Words that indicate you may be over-generalizing are: all, every, none, never, always, everybody, and nobody. (McKay, 1981:20)

In the above peanut butter and jelly example, "I always get overwhelmed when making food," the over-generalization made by the observer is stuck to the inner child and is frozen in time (age-regressed) and then over-generalized to limit life. Rather than learning how to cook, the child within a man might hire a cook or insist his spouse do the cooking. This limits the adult in present time.

3. Relationship Confusion

Over-generalization is often present in relationships. The child learns that confusion is a powerful tool to push people away, to get space for himself or get taken care of. Let us imagine that the little boy, when asked to do anything, looks as if he doesn't quite understand. Dad then shows him how it is done. Next, Mom asks the little boy to change the light bulb in the lamp. The son acts bewildered and responds with a look of confusion. Mom then takes over and does the task. The well-known comedian Bill Cosby would say, that Dads know how to act stupid, knowing that the Mom will rescue them. Actually, it is the little boy inside of the man which has learned to act stupid to get Mom to do it for him.

After a while a child learns that looking, acting, or being confused causes someone to take care of him. This is a classic example because, once placed on automatic, the confused act or identity appears real and is supported by the social or family network that reinforces its existence. This form of confusion is more situation oriented. The therapy must center on the trance of confusion, which is being used by the inner child to hypnotize the adult in present time.

An example of utilizing this strategy involves a case where a young girl was sexually molested. In adulthood she now experiences a fear response when relating to men. First, there were several trance phenomena the child created. Inner voices, dialogues, blocking-out, etc. are created during a period of confusion or chaos.

Second, the trigger is "men." The inner child's response becomes the problem. Thus, automatic creation of all men as the abuser must be changed as part of the therapy, in order to shift the subjective experience of the client (see Appendix, The Trigger).

4. Control Confusion

In the fourth confusion technique, the observer, through a series of interactions, creates confusion in his/her environment. This is a protective, defensive stance, which can afford the child a subtle sense of safety and control over interactions that usually afford little control. In this style the individual learns how to outsmart and out-maneuver the environment by creating confusion. The child learns that by using certain words, talking over the adult's head, using or being a certain way, the adults remain bewildered, even stand-offish. This helps the child to feel powerful when they actually feel *powerless*. The child actually feels powerless, overwhelmed and confused and, in that confusion, the child decides to confuse others in order to feel powerful.

There is an old axiom in Gestalt therapy that says, "Do unto others that which was done unto you." Let's look at the last example in the possible light of one of the most powerful hypnotherapists in history, Milton H. Erickson, M.D. Erickson had polio and suffered strokes. He developed ways to help control pain and developed inner resources to survive. He then used these methods (do unto others) to help multitudes of people. One of Erickson's major contributions to the field of hypnosis, according to Jeffery Zeig, Ph.D., was in the area of *confusion*. Erickson was not only a master of pain control, but a master of inducing confusion with clients. It is the opinion of this author that Erickson, as would anyone who suffered from polio and strokes, went through deep powerlessness, confusion, and chaos, which were time frozen. He then utilized that state and did unto others that which was done unto him; created confusion in others. He used this, however, to help people by-pass conscious interference and helped them feel powerful when they complained of feeling powerless in their lives. Erickson could also feel powerful inducing confusion in others, which was done unto him. This would enable Erickson to counter his own feelings of powerlessness by keeping others "one down," and himself "one up." This was the creative genius of Erickson, utilizing his own process of confusion to help empower others and himself.

When creation of confusion to handle powerlessness is placed on automatic, however, the individual begins to experience feelings of isolation, alienation, being misunderstood and loneliness, because to maintain the feeling of power and control, a person must continue to create confusion in others and in his own world.

Often the overly-intellectual person will use the above strategy. One patient would always confuse his parents and impact his environment and relationships to gain a sense of control. People who feel they must always be *one-up*, subtly placing others *one-down*, suffer from this trance. It is the resistance to feeling powerless or *one-down* that the child within the adult finds abhorrent. Therefore, to not feel *one-down*, the strategy of creating confusion is employed. A confusion approach can work, but loneliness is a high price paid for control, particularly when the devices are so imbedded in the child within the adult, who no longer experiences choice. This protective trance is automatic and out of the person's control. The adult suffering from this inner child's trance does not know why he turns people off. This is the power of the trance of the inner child.

The Next Step
Handling Confusion

1. *Allowing the confusion.* The first approach involves allowing yourself to be fully confused, and continue to feel and create the con-fusion. What is paramount in this process is (1) continue breathing and notice where or what part of the body feels tight, and (2) tighten the body and coordinate it with the holding of breath. In this way, experience a *whole* body awareness of the confusion and how it relates to the rest of the body. It is through intentionally experiencing and creating confusion that the observer can wake-up to present time and not use the inner child window any longer.

2. *Differentiate.* As with all trances, confusion is experienced in a block, as one, undifferentiated mass. Notice in detail the specific areas of the confusion, and assign different adjectives, such as clear, dry, open, dark, cloudy, smothering. This shifts the experience, which brings forth a different subjective feeling.

Handling Interpersonal Confusion

1. *The Extension of Vision or Perceptional Field.*

   This technique includes utilizing the entire experience of confusion, by watching or witnessing the confusion just "as it is," with no judgment or desire to remove it. By allowing and experiencing confusion, a shift in consciousness occurs.

2. *Witnessing and Measuring.*

   In a repetitive fashion, ask yourself the following questions, writing down your answers.

   a. Where is the confusion?
   b. What is the shape of the con-fusion?
   c. Is it vague or clear?
   d. Does it have a color?
   e. Does it change how I feel about myself?
   f. Does it change how I feel about the world?
      By repeating these questions again and again, the confusion is witnessed.
   g. Notice that you are the observer and creator of the con-fusion.

Conclusion

In this culture individuals attempt to "break through," "get clear" of their con-fusion. Paradoxically, trying to get clear resists the confusion. An I-dentity whose goal is to get clear is created. The most interesting facet of this resides in the "getting clear" process. The child resists experiencing the trance of confusion. Simply put, trying to "get clear," "understand," "find out," or "know," is a way the child within the adult resists confusion. Thus trying to get rid of the confusion keeps it present. This resistance to experiencing the experience of confusion, along with the label "confusion is bad," keeps the trance frozen. Individuals can learn to take responsibility for the creation of confusion and become more willing to experience it without the resistance of trying to "get clear." Being with the confusion, creating it *intentionally,* or *choosing* it in present time, allows its frozen stuckness to shift, thus freeing the adult from the inner child's clutches and awakening the *observer* and creator of confusion.

•11

Trance Dreaming

Dream... Dream ... Dream...Dream...
Dream ...Dream ... Dream...Dream...
When I want you
In the night
When I need you
To hold me tight
Whenever I want you
All I have to do is dream

Everly Brothers

Trance dreaming occurs as the *observer* disconnects the child from the family or world. The child loses itself as it begins to *dream*. Actually, this is the purpose of the dream: to create a better world inside, to handle the pain of outside. Unfortunately, the child who is dreaming remains time frozen; the *observer* creates a dream within the child that likewise is disconnected from the world. In other words, in order to dream the child disconnects from the world and disconnects from the body. This trance, which is created by the *observer*, disconnects the child and is the way the child now survives.

The problem is that the dream is frozen within the child and is therefore distorted, because it resonates from the child's world, not the adult present world. The inner child dreams of being a knight in shining armor rescuing damsels in distress. Once this is placed on automatic, the dream continues in present time as if it were real. Co-dependent men or women, who dream of saving their partner from their addiction, are in the trance of dreaming. In order to dream, they not only disconnect from their partner's problem (drinking), they also disconnect from their own bodies. When this occurs, the child within the adult chooses the dream in the 1992 world. As the observer sleeps, the child within the adult cannot understand why the dream is not manifesting. Furthermore, the child within the adult holds so tightly to the dream that she may try to get the drinker to match the dream. This trance of the inner child can be *so intense* that the dream continually gets chosen over present time reality.

I worked with a woman who was so love addicted to an abusive man that the child within's dream would not let go. After years of therapy, she continually chose the dream rather than the reality; she dreamed he would change. (*He never has*). I mention this example because she never gave up the dream, or the abusive man, so intense was her inner child's trance.

This dream now comes from the child within the adult, not the present time *observer*. The task is to wake-up the present time observer from the past time child identity that is dreaming. This is done with the following exercises:

1. Ask yourself where in your body you feel the child who is dreaming.
2. Intentionally create a dream and place it inside the body part where the dreaming child resides.
3. Notice the difference between you and the inner child's dream.
4. Create the dreaming child several times.

The dream is deeply layered in the child and often becomes a major, motivational impetuous for the adult, as a lifestyle or rationale for ongoing behavior. For example, in the classic Woody Allen film *Play It Again, Sam*, Woody dreams he is like Humphrey Bogart. The exaggeration of the dream makes it obvious that the child within is dreaming. Problems arise for the character because he can never be himself; he is always trying to be Humphrey Bogart (his dream). The unaware adult imagines the dream is real, not realizing the child within has created this idealized dream.

Difficulty for the adult stems from the fact that she is unaware that her dream is a trance, coming from the little child, because the dream seems logical. The dream trance can be supported, argued, and discussed with rational prowess and emotional logic. In the case of Woody Allen, he argues that being like Bogart is how you're supposed to be in order to get the relationship you want. How many of us have a dream that tells us if we look, act or are a certain way, we will have the relationship of our *dreams*? This is the problem in many of my couple's sessions. One or both members of the relationship have an inner child's dream. Sometimes the spouse tries to get the partner to change to fit the dream. Sometimes the dream is so idealized that the adult with a dreaming inner child suffers greatly. The work begins with my asking the adult to look at the inner child's dream rather than trying to change the spouse. The tragedy of this common situation is that the spouse never experiences the present-time relationship. The idealized dream is overlaid on top of *what is*.

It must be recognized, while working with oneself, that there are feelings of grief, disillusionment, discontent, and general emotional confusion, when past dreams are confronted. The present world does not match the child within's dream, which has solidified in the adult.

Trance dreams are important for many reasons. Certain people do not daydream. Being unable to dream, daydream, or fantasize becomes a liability, because the ability to access one's intuition is cut off. The opposite is also true; a trance dream on automatic creates disconnections from now, since it is the child within who stops and starts the trance, rather than the observer in present time. In the former, the inner child dreams; in the latter, the inner child is hypervigilant.

An example is the man I was seeing for counseling who did not daydream. Since he had no daydreaming ability, he was experiencing a focused, over-identified state with high anxiety and hypervigilance. He didn't have the ability to let go and trance dream. In this case, his inner child had to be hypervigilant because his father had been institutionalized as a child for emotional problems. Like the overidentified trance, trance dreaming equaled disaster.

With the observer asleep, a trance dream is one way the child within the adult resists experiencing the present. Health lies in the ability to create trance dreams and cease creating them, *at choice.* For most people their trance dreams are on automatic and are versions of unfinished childhood themes. *Choice* is the ability to pick up or put down trance dreams, at will. An example is the woman who said, "There are beings/guides who come to me, and I'm going to be like Christ." I outgrew my own dream of playing basketball. Her dream solidified. Years go by and she forgets that she is a little child in the dreams. Now she is 30 and not ready to live the dream. A critical shift in viewpoint is required; the old dream puts her in conflict with the reality of today. At this point the therapist starts bringing the dream into a level of reality organization, i.e., what's real and what's not real, in present time.

If you do not dream or have interrupted your dreaming, it's critical to work with yourself to develop the skill of trance dreaming; this interrupts the inner child's hypervigilant identity. Some creative ideas will come out of this new skill. Self-interruptions, invented in childhood, undermine peoples' ability to dream. Parents give many suggestions when they say, "Be realistic," which means, "See the world the way I see it." The child stops himself from ever really going into his own dream state.

The Identity Dream

Look at me
Who am I supposed to be
Who am I supposed to be
Look at me
What am I supposed to do
What am I supposed to do
Who are we
Oh, my love

John Lennon

Identity distortion is a time frozen story of what happened or a general story that is created to resist the trauma of present time. In the dream people listen to him and see him. For example, a friend of mine, that I lived with in India, was abused as a child. During the trauma of abuse he dreamed of being at the United Nations, giving a talk on the World's problems and being loved and listened to.

Problems arise when the identity distortion becomes context-independent, or when the identity distortion becomes stuck and begins to function autonomously, without regard for interpersonal feedback from the family, school, or relationships. As an example, a child with no musical ability who imagines himself being admired as a rock and roll star operates without interpersonal feedback. It is the interpersonal feedback that enables the self-to-self trance of the child within to be questioned, so that the observer can let go of its creation. Developmentally, without appropriate interpersonal interactions, the trance becomes more solid. To move smoothly through this developmental experience, requires an appropriate interpersonal environment. The identity dream, acting child-to-child without appropriate feedback interpersonally, might cause depression, anxiety, etc.

"Externalization" occurs when an individual, during his development, is denied the particular experience of a safe, loving, supportive environment that would afford him a sense of whole-ness, completion and well-being. To counter or neutralize this deprivation, he creates a dream character who gives him the complete experience required for a greater sense of self. Children that develop imaginary playmates who provide them with appropriate levels of love, understanding, and affection demonstrate this phenomenon.

Externalization is a process that provides a person with disconnected experiences that are needed. To repeat the earlier example, while I lived in India, an introverted friend had a recurring identity dream of himself delivering a speech on the state of the World to the United Nations. After chatting with him for a while, I mentioned that nobody had listened to him as a child and he had been abused, hence, his inner child created this United Nations dream. Here, the family was transferred by the inner child onto the United Nations.

The problem arises as the dream, friend, lover, prince, situation, etc., begins to be projected onto the external world. This externalization process becomes a compulsive tendency to finish interpersonally (with the world) what needs to be completed with yourself. In other words, since you were never listened to, you compulsively try to get yourself understood. This phenomenon becomes a problem because the projections occur in the child-like state. Consequently, the age-regressed adult can only interact as a child attempting to complete itself, rather than as an adult meeting its needs.

For example, the child within my friend went into a child-like state, dreaming of people listening to him, rather than as an adult actually asking people to listen to him. The dream of the inner-child prevented him from asking for and getting his present-time needs met.

The Next Step
Handling Trance Dreaming

Too much Daydreaming?

1. Notice the dream.
2. Notice where the inner child who is dreaming is in your body.
3. Create a dream, and put it inside the child in the body.
4. Create the child and the dream.
5. See the difference between you (observer/creator) and the dreaming child.

Facilitating Trance Dreaming

This exercise is constructed to facilitate dreaming for people who are unable to experience this phenomenon, or for people that are hypervigilant.

Step 1—Relax. Move into a comfortable place and begin to imagine different, pleasurable scenes: woods, mountains, oceans, favorite people, etc.

Step 2 - Notice. Notice the entire scene to its outer edges.

Step 3 - Experience. Step into the scene, and feel what it feels like to be a part of the dream.

Step 4 - Before Bed. Prior to going to sleep, ask yourself to allow dreams to happen and be remembered. Sometimes people report asking for solutions to problems and receiving the answer, utilizing this technique. As an exercise, write down the first conscious thought upon awakening. The accuracy or insight of the communication may be a surprise.

All these exercises facilitate the increased skill and awareness of hypnotic dreaming, to aid in self-understanding.

Summary

What cannot be over-emphasized is that dreams are *not wrong*. They are disruptive when they get out of control and act automatically because the child within the adult loses the present-time world and the connection to the body. It is by observing and creating knowingly, that allows the *observer/creator* to wake-up and get "in charge" of the dreaming rather than be a prisoner of the inner child's trance.

Handling Identity Dreams

1. *Acknowledge.* Watch the mind acknowledge different stories and themes that arise.
2. *Notice.* Notice, for example, (a) rags to riches: seeing oneself arising from an impoverished position to become recognized and acknowledged (*Rocky*-type movies); (b) Cinderella complex: dreaming someone will materialize and take you "away from all this"; (c) seeing self as a football or rock star, or an influential person. Notice the story line; what is usually seen in these identity dreams is a *one-dimensional replica* of the story. Notice that you are the *observer* of the inner child's dream.

3. Ask yourself what needs the inner child is trying to fulfill through dreaming." Write down your answers.
4. Ask yourself, "Am I willing to ask for my needs in my present-time relationships?" Write down your unfulfilled needs and whether you are willing to begin to ask for them directly. Try this for a week, and write down what feelings arose and how others' responded to you. For example, if you ask for affection this week, fear might arise. Also, how did you see others respond to your direct request?

Summary

Identity dreaming, a sub-set of dreaming, aids the individual during times of stress. It is only a problem when the inner child acts autonomously and treats the present as the past, outside of the control and awareness of the sleeping *observer*.

•12

Amnesia

Amnesia, often referred to as denial, is a trance that can operate on its own without the adult's conscious control in present time. The child within, experiences this trance as a way of protecting himself from uncomfortable situations.* Here are several styles of amnesia.

1. *Self-deceptive amnesia*, manifests when the child within the adult forgets to remember a situation. An example of this might be an adult child of an alcoholic who forgets his parent's drinking.
2. *Deletion*, or leaving out appropriate information during communicative interactions, allows a non-committal statement that could be interpreted in a variety of ways. Simple statements like, "You know how it feels when things happen." What feels, who feels, what happens?
3. *Forgetting*, Amnesia occurs when the individual forgets what he said as an attempt to control a situation he perceives as uncontrollable. This denial pattern occurs when a person agrees to something to reduce tension, and then forgets they agreed to it.

---

* Although this is not the place to discuss it in depth, severe amnesia can be a signpost for dissociative disorders or even multiple personality disorder.

These amnesic states are the *observer's* intense efforts to keep the child in balance. They are exhibited by forgetting information or events to control uncontrollable situations, usually relating to former experiences like chaos, emptiness, or feeling out of control or overwhelmed.

As an example, children from dysfunctional families often feel overwhelmed, lost, abandoned or afraid. To handle that, the *observer* creates caretakers, lost children, and enabler identities, which are covered with amnesia so the person does not remember how this identity was brought about. Identities are created by the *observer* to handle chaos. If amnesia (What happened?) is used, it surrounds the identity and the reason the coping device was formed is not remembered, (i.e., the trauma).

Amnesia is forgetting, and it is a defense. Amnesia developed because the *observer* did not want the child to remember. If someone comes into therapy and says, "Hey, I just can't remember!," she also exhibits symptoms such as stopping her breath and holding her muscles, in order to maintain the forgetting. Amnesia is a defense, a way that the *observer* helped the child to survive the circumstances in which she grew up.

When a client verbalizes, "I have the worst memory in the world, and I'd like to work on it," or, "I can't remember what happened, but I sense I was sexually molested," then the strategy for a therapist is very simple. Have them breathe and look at you. This will access the "forgotten" experience. Patterns are held in the body and breath. This is why I suggest that traumatized clients receive some form of body therapy: Rolfing, Bio-Energetics, Feldenkrais, Alexander or massage.

Body memories of trauma are buried in the body. Body work helps the "forgotten" or denied memory stored in the body to emerge. Furthermore, many schools of psychotherapy, i.e. Reichian, Bioenergetic, suggest that a body pattern correlates with a psychological pattern.

Working with Yourself

Do your breathing and your muscles stay the same? Almost every psychological component seems to have a physical component. If you are directed to breathe, look and stay aware; the events that precipitated the amnesia often emerge. There's nothing wrong with having amnesia, if you are able to pick and choose when you want it. The following is an edited transcript that demonstrates work with amnesia.

Stephen:	I want you to remember a time ... do you remember a time when you felt real amnesic?
Patient:	Yes, I don't remember getting beat up by a bully in school.
Stephen:	As you see an image of yourself in that situation, I'd like you to see that bully; describe him, and feel the "you" in the image inside your body. (I am asking the client to return the trauma back inside his body.) What happens to your body for you to accomplish that? (The symptom then emerges.)
Stephen:	Tell me what happens if you imagine yourself in a real situation where you were frustrated, but you could not remember. Can you see that kind of an image?
Patient:	Yes.
Stephen:	If you were to pull it back inside of your body, what happens?
Patient:	I feel stupid.
Stephen:	You feel stupid, and what is happening in your body and to your muscles?
Patient:	I'm giving it all, holding back right there (stomach area).

Stephen:	(To Class. She already gave you a clue to an inner dialogue.) Did you hear what you said? (feeling stupid)
Patient:	I didn't hear what I said.
Stephen:	Did you hear what she said? (To another student)
Student:	Yes.
Stephen:	Did you?
Patient:	No.
Stephen:	Living proof of amnesia!
Patient:	It's not true. (Laughter)
Stephen:	There's an example of your amnesia. I learn from everyone I work with. "TEACH ME HOW THE INNER CHILD CREATES THE SYMPTOM," is the message I give the client. I learn how to work with people just by staying in this kind of a process.

Hypermnesia

Hypermnesia is remembering everything. That also is a defense, a way the organism helps itself to survive. In my family, my parents were inconsistent. I listened to every word they uttered and remembered what they said. Then a year or six months later, they would say, "I told you to do this," and I would correct them. They would say "God, I can't believe what a memory you have. You can remember everything," which, of course, was the perfect suggestion for hypermnesia. I could hold them to what they had said 20 years before, 10 years before, five years before. I remembered every single word. The negative side of hypermnesia is a watchful, mistrusting attitude, like hypervigilance.

The Next Step
Handling Amnesia

1. Locate where in the body the inner child identity is.
2. Ask the inner child questions like, "What can you (the inner child) remember about X" (a particular situation).

For example, if you have an idea that your father drank, ask the inner child, "What can you (inner child) not remember about father's drinking?" or "What do you (the inner child) not know about your childhood?" Write down your answers and keep asking the question, until nothing pops-up.

Examples for remembering the past: "What do you (the inner child) not know about X?" Write down your answers until nothing more pops up.

Fill in X with the words below, and keep asking the questions, writing them down, until nothing pops-up.

My mother
My father
My brother/sister
My childhood
My relationship

Examples for remembering current events:

My business
My car
My bills
My life

Other examples:

1. What are you (the inner child), unwilling to know about the past?

2. What are you (the inner child), willing to know about the past?
3. What did you (the inner child), decide to know about the past?
4. What did you (the inner child), decide to not know about the past?

You hold a volume of information; one way to break beliefs about what you can and can't remember is to *ask* ... and *notice* what occurs.

Conclusion

Understanding that both amnesia and hypermnesia are reactions to environmental, unwanted, family situations, makes it easy to undo the not knowing (denial) and *expand* the knowing. This gives you more choice or range in the experiences of the world and allows the resources of your past to open to you.

Once the past is open, an individual can use it as a resource library of forgotten material, which can be taken into the present and future. Denying incidents of the past takes a lot of energy, energy that could be used in present time relationships. Removing the not knowing provides more energy in present-time with which to know and be creative.

•13

Sensory Distortion: I Can't Feel

As soon as you're born they make you feel small
by giving you no time instead of it all
Till the pain is so big you feel nothing at all.
                    "Working Class Hero" John Lennon

Sensory distortion is a trance state experienced as numbness, pain, dullness, or as the opposite, hypersensitivity. Three types of sensory distortion include:

1. *Emotional sensory distortion*: is a defense to protect the *observer* creates numbness within the child. For example, the child develops numbness during an incident of child abuse. Years later the child within the adult develops a numbness or lack of sexual sensations.
2. *Hypersensitivity* occurs when someone is overly sensitive to the world. For example, an individual walks into

a room and the child within the adult imagines everyone is talking about him or someone shows up 15
minutes late and the child within personalizes it, thinking, "Why me?"

3. *Sensory distortion and pain* is a trance that shrinks the
focus of attention to only the pained area. For example,
if a person has a headache, the attention of the individual is focused on the head. The goal would be to
expand the focus of attention to include the whole
body.

Below are cases that illustrate methods of working with oneself,
and are guides to the next step of dismantling the inner child's
automatic sensory distortion, and awakening the *observer*.

Type 1 - Emotional Sensory Distortion

A 250-pound man came to see me. He requested therapy for
obesity. As we began the therapy, he spaced out, disconnected and
then felt his body was like a stone (sensory distortion). He had no
sensations. I suggested he feel a sensation and then experience a
space, and another sensation and a short space, and a sensation and
a long space. (There are spaces that often go unnoticed between
sensations). Eventually, the undifferentiated mass (his body) began
to throb or pulsate. He began to take charge of the "rock-dead"
feeling of protection and lengthened or shortened the gaps or spaces
between sensations, by himself. Lengthening the gap would slow or
lessen the sensations, shortening the gap heightened sensations.
The result for the client was increased energy and a greater "feeling
of his body," instead of his old pattern of withdrawal into denial, to
avoid sensation.

Type II — Hypersensitive Distortion

The second type of sensory distortion, hypersensitivity, is
illustrated by a woman who felt hypersensitive in groups of people.
She experienced rapid sensations in her heart and chest. As in the
first type of sensory distortion, the speeding up or slowing down of
sensations altered her subjective experience. She imagined people
were thinking bad thoughts of her. Once again I asked her to create
a sensation and notice the space, and create another sensation and

notice the space. In this way, the *observer* took charge of creating the sensations.

Another style of hypersensitivity comes from cognitive therapy and is called *Personalizing*.

> Personalizing is the tendency to relate everything around you to yourself. A recently married man thinks that every time his wife talks about tiredness she means she is tired of him. A man whose wife complains about rising prices hears the complaints as attacks on his ability as a breadwinner. A major aspect of personalizing is the habit of comparing yourself to others. He's dumb, I'm smart. The underlying assumption is that your worth is questionable. The basic thinking error in personalization is that you interpret each experience, each conversation, each look as a clue to your worth and value. (McKay, 1981:21)

When I'm late, my partner personalizes, "He doesn't love me." Somebody doesn't like my seminar, and I ask, "What did I do wrong?" When you are not personalizing, you realize this partner is always late, it doesn't pertain to me, or this person always says bad things about everyone. It's not just me. It's not *personal*.

The personalizing style of hypersensitivity comes from a parent who is personalizing. For example, I worked with a woman who personalized everything her husband said. If her husband said, "I'm mad at you," she would go into the inner child identity and feel like there was something wrong with her. The key to this understanding is that in order to personalize you have to age-regress and become the wounded inner child and treat present time as if it were the past. If you are an *observer* in present time, you will see the, "I'm mad at you," is coming from your husbands' "stuff" and not personal to you.

Type III — Sensory Distortion, Energy Dispersal

Anesthesia is used to control pain. Two cases illustrate this phenomenon. A woman presented herself for therapy with chronic neck pain. The emotional material that emerged was a child-like feeling, "The world is going to collapse." I asked, "Where does the experience of sensation feel sharper? Where does the experience of sensations feel duller?" Using the word "sensation" helps to shift the focus from pain to "sensation." I continued, "Where are the pain sensations burning? Where are they cooler?" All trances fail to utilize all of the experience. The goal is to offer suggestions of recognition for other sensory experiences, so the subjective experience shifts or varies slightly.

> *Principle VIII*: The greater variability offered any problem, the less it remains fixed.

A second example deals with localized sensations manifesting in a particular area, such as headaches. A woman came to therapy with a migraine headache. First I had her see the headache as sensations. Then I suggested, "Just as sensations can move from your right index finger to your elbow, or your right toe into your ankle, if you focus your attention *now,* you might...let me know when the sensations begin to move from your head into your neck, not to mention (nice way to suggest) into your arms and hands." Eventually by this sequencing, the sensations became equally distributed all over her body, relieving the headache.

By suggesting movement of the sensations, you reconnect foreground (headache) to the body (background), and expand the focus of attention to include the whole body. The trance of sensory distortion is shifted. Stated more simply, the "A"-tension is only experienced in the head. The task is to expand awareness so that the attention is on the whole body.

> *Principle IX*: Without shrinking the focus of attention, there can be no trance; and without a trance, the symptom cannot be held together.

Another example is a client who claimed he had only emotional pain in his life, and it focused in his stomach.

I suggested that he might experience a desirable sensation in his hand or foot. He nodded. "And a painful sensation in another part of your body?" Nod. "A pleasant sensation in another part of the body?" Nod. "A pleasant sensation in another part?" Over time, by offering opposite or desirable sensations, we expanded his focus of attention, and he experienced himself in a varied way. To enhance his experience after the pleasant and unpleasant sensations were equal or balanced, I suggested that he notice the sensations moving. They moved into one another, merging and creating an integrated experience of both. This integration of pleasant and unpleasant experiences yielded a third experience of sensation, which was not available earlier.

The Next Step
Handling Sensory Distortion

1. Speed up or slow down the sensations, or expand and contract gaps between two sensations.
2. Differentiate the pain sensations by suggesting different sensations like sharp, burning, light, etc.
3. Suggest dispersing the sensations (energy) through the body equally.
4. Suggest to yourself a pleasant sensation in a safe area, and an unpleasant sensation in another area.

Questioning the Inner Child's
Sensory Distortion

1. Locate where in your body the inner child lives, the child that is having the trance of sensory distortion.
2. Dialogue with the inner child, asking the following questions, and writing down the answers that pop-up.
   a. What are you (the inner child) willing to feel?
   b. What are you (the inner child) unwilling to feel?
   c. What are you (the inner child) willing to experience?
   d. What are you (the inner child) unwilling to experience?
   e. What have you (the inner child) decided to feel?
   f. What have you (the inner child) decided not to feel?
   g. What sensations are you (the inner child) willing to have?

h. What sensations are you (the inner child) unwilling to have?
i. From what incident(s) or trauma(s) is the numbness protecting you (the inner child)?

In each case write down your answers.

Conclusion

Sensory distortion, the slowing down or speeding up of sensations, is a creative act of the observer. Once the sensory distortion
is seen for what it is, with no judgments, labels, or evaluation, the
observer can take over its creative function, which it had given to
the inner child. The inner child *automatically* had contracted or
expanded sensations. Now the *observer* can own its creative side
and exist in present time. Learning what occurred to the child that
caused the sensory distortion (numbness) helps free up the psyche-
energy holding the memory, the trauma, and the accompanying
frozen sensations.

•14

Spiritualizing

Now that I showed you what I've been through,
Don't take nobody's word for what you can do,

There ain't no Jesus goin' come from the sky,
Now that I found out, I know I can cry.
I ... I found out.
I ... I found out.

Old Hare Krishna's got nothin on you,
Just keep you crazy ... with nothin to do,
Keep you occupied with pie in the sky,
There ain't no Guru can see thru your eyes,
I ... I found out
I ... I found this out ....

"I Found Out" John Lennon

Preamble

Before I discuss spiritualizing and its effects, it is important for me to emphasize several points.

First, what prevents a true communion with the underlying unity is our automatic trances. Secondly, the intention of this section is to free us all from the past and age-regressed world views, which inhibit our experience of this underlying unity. Third, what we are left with is uninterrupted awareness uninhibited by memory, distortion, resistance to chaos, or in a word, trances. It is with this pure, uninterrupted awareness, without prior automatic trances, that the natural interconnection and unity becomes more available. This natural unity, called "quantum consciousness" is what I believe to be a natural spirituality. A spirituality where we are free to be separate and free to feel the interconnection of everything as a choice, rather than automatic separation or automatic fusion, which can be mistaken for unity.

While I travel and train individuals in my workshops I am often asked, "What makes for a good client or practitioner in this style of work?" My reply is always the same; 1) a willingness to look at and confront whatever stands in the way of this unity consciousness, 2) a willingness to let go of belief structures no matter how "comfortable", and 3) awareness, which I have called the solvent to the glue of trance states, the *trance*-ending ingredient.

This is the attitude, a warrior's attitude, of being called to be aware, to confront and let go of concepts, many of which have never been looked at as concepts, but assumed to be *truths*.

To illustrate this let me narrate a story of what happened to me in India in about 1979. I was visiting my teacher, Nisargadatta Maharaj. He asked me, "Do you know yourself?" I replied, "I feel a lot of love and bliss, and I can even see energy." He snarled back, "I'm not interested in knowing if you are *satisfied* or *pacified* with your spiritual life, do you know yourself?" I said, "no." He said, "Then shut your mouth." Two years later I appreciated what he was so dramatically saying. You must not be *pacified* with your *spiritual game*, rather you must confront and dismantle your spiritual beliefs and the spiritual structures of your mind to find out *who you are*. To do this, and with this in mind, let us explore the trance of spiritualizing.

Spiritualizing

One of the most involved and intricate trances of the inner child is "spiritualizing." The spiritualizing trance develops as an infant and moves through several normal, developmental phases. This chapter will explore the processes of these developmental phases and show how they can lead the child to the trance I call spiritualizing. I distinguish three phases of development and call them first, second, and third level processes.

The first level begins as the infant believes that she creates her parents' actions or, what is commonly called in the psychological world, "magical thinking." In the second level, the child *idealizes* the parent. In the third phase, an infant makes the parents into gods and goddesses. Spiritualizing, then, is the third of these levels.

To understand what I mean by spiritualizing it is essential to look first at what are known traditionally in psychotherapy as primary and secondary processes. Let's look at an infant just around the time of birth and through the first several years of development.

First Level Processes

First level processes involve basic cognitions or understandings that an infant internally develops and later generalizes to the world. Cognitive trance structures produce understandings for the infant in the development of the inner child identity. This trance understanding carries over to how the child views himself, his parents, God and the workings of the universe.

This developmental process from infant to child is noted here so we can question basic assumptions we have about life and see them as *just assumptions*. Questioning our world view, or shall I say the world view of the infant/child identity which is the window we habitually look through, enables us to dispel age-regressed limitations and move closer to the pure awareness of the observer uninhibited by personal trances.

For example, when a child believes she always should be taken care of, frustration ensues when the child within an adult hypnotizes the adult into believing she is *entitled* to be taken care of. The assumption, "I'm supposed to be taken care of," diminishes personal responsibility and power. As the adult matures, they can become conservative, politically, and the adult can believe, "the rich and powerful will take care of the rest of us." The problem is the rich and powerful take care of themselves, leaving our inner children feeling victimized. Cognizing that the rich and powerful will "trickle down" money to us is a trance of the inner child, and a fusion with Mom and Dad. This keeps the present-time adult from feeling empowered.

Three Basic First Level Processes

1. *I created it*: This trance relates to the beliefs the infant develops when he is born, opens his eyes, and sees Mom, Dad, nurse, doctor, etc. What is cognized? "I created Mom and Dad." The infant believes this, and often this belief is carried into adulthood. The results, as we will explore later, are paramount to the development of a self-view, a world view and the adaptation of a spiritual philosophy.

2. *Infantile grandiosity*: The baby feels cold and Mom or Dad places a blanket on her. Next, baby thinks hungry, and Mom or Dad brings food. Next, baby sensates, "I want to be picked up." Somebody comes and picks up the baby. What is cognized? "I created them to come and take care of me."

These two processes of the first level of development are often referred to as "magical thinking": I created them to come and pick me up, my thoughts create or my thoughts make others respond. This is grandiose because it appears to the infant that his thoughts are so powerful they create or bring about external reality.

Adult Problem State: Obsessive thinking. When Mom or Dad do not come to fill the infant's wants or needs, the infant cognizes something new. Sometimes a child believes that if it *thinks harder, more or visualizes someone coming, they will come.* The illusion is that they control Mom and Dad with their thoughts. Obsessive thinking is a control issue and touches on *magical thinking*. "If I think hard enough about it, it will happen." Recently some new age thinkers have countered the obvious discrepancy between thinking and outcome with the contention that there must be some other thought or counter-intention which is preventing your thought from manifesting. This leads to a new age philosophy that promotes letting go of the thought or belief that interferes with manifesting what you want. The unquestioned presupposition, *thoughts create reality.* This will be discussed later.

Adult Problem State: Trying to control others through thought, imagining you can control others' behavior through thought or by acting a certain way.

Adult Problem State: Self blame. "It must be my fault that things didn't work out." It's my fault if someone doesn't like me." Both these strategies give the person an illusion of control over others' behavior, even if they are counterproductive or self-destructive strategies.

3. In addition to "I created it" and *grandiosity*, another first level process is reinforcement. In this stage the basic mind structures of the infant are re-enforced by the world so the developing infant believes its original world view to be correct. This occurs when a dysfunctional family reinforces a behavior, like smiling or being passive. The family responds to the child when it doesn't need anything. The parents seem happy. The child decides or cognizes that smiling will get her needs met, not anger nor actions.

Adult Problem State: "I create how others feel about me," or the variation, "I am responsible for what others think or feel about me." This begins early and the *grandiosity* and *magical thinking* are re-enforced by Mom/Dad making statements like, "You *make* me angry." The child believes the behavioral and verbal feedback and continues the illusion that he creates how people feel or interact.

Adult Problem State: Over-responsibility: "I am responsible for others' experience, and I am responsible for what people think or feel about me."

Adult Problem State: Loss of Boundary: "It must have been something I did that caused them not to like me. This *infantile trance* has a pre-verbal assumption that two people are merged. For example, the infant sees herself and mom as one. In a relationship years later when the other wants to be separate, the infantile trance pops up leaving the adult confused and possibly with a fear of separation.

Spiritualizing is a new way of looking at the defense system that occurs years later as the infant defends himself from being separate.

Adult Problem State: Loss of self, giving up oneself to get love. Often children give up their power, ideas, etc. to get love from their parents. The child believes, "I control them (parents) by controlling my feelings. If I can control my feelings, I can control their feelings. I'm in charge." Picture a child who becomes angry, and in response, the parents get angry to control the child. The child controls and represses his anger. The parents smile and give him a hug. From the point of view of the child, by controlling his behavior, he can control others' behaviors and how others feel about him. This is the resistance to being out of control or powerless. *Grandiosity* resists the perceived chaos of powerlessness that the child experienced. The child cannot acknowledge its powerlessness so, to regain a state of power, he cognizes he is responsible and in charge of how others feel about him. "If I control my thoughts, feelings or actions, I can control *their* reactions, thoughts, or feelings about me.

Often with incest survivors, the child creates beliefs like, "I made it happen." If I'm seductive, it will happen; if I'm not, it won't. I'm in charge of turning him/her on." or "I'm special because I am so powerful." All of these cognitions resist the powerlessness of the situation. The child, to avoid the chaos and pain, goes into a trance of making herself feel powerful, in charge, rather than acknowledging she was powerless, and the abuser was in charge. The cognition helps protect her from being overwhelmed by the emotions of powerlessness, feeling helpless, and victimization.

Adult Problem State: Rigidity. Here the adult is being hypnotized by the inner child to control his feelings, thoughts, and expressions as a way to be loved. Often the child within the adult will try to control everyone else's feelings, thoughts, or expressions. Their emotional rigidity prevents them from feeling their vulnerability and need for love. The rigidity allows them to believe they can live without love, or can withdraw love to control people.

The developing infant re-enforces her cognitions, beliefs, and strategies in an attempt to organize her world. More simply put, when facing her dysfunctional situation, the child employs survival strategies to defend herself from the fear of annihilation.

Second Level Processes

The second level of development is "idealizing." The developing child creates his parents as ideals, in order to avoid facing the terror of death, chaos, or annihilation. For example in a house where one or both parents are dysfunctional, the child does not have the strength to face the chaos which he views as possible death through neglect or abuse. The *observer* has the child go into a trance to not feel, not see, or not know what the situation is. The *observer* creates the child idealizing the parents and creates them as perfect. This helps the child resist the chaos of seeing them as dysfunctional and provides him with a strategy to handle his own internal chaos. If he saw his parents' dysfunction, it would be too horrifying; so idealization seems like the only sane path.

Adult Problem State: Years later in relationships, the inner child within the adult idealizes her spouse. This prevents the present time adult from seeing her spouse in present time. Sometimes the inner child will idealize to the degree of only seeing, or falling in love with, the *potential* or *imagined ideal* of the spouse.

In other words the child within the adult uses the trance with the spouse that worked with the parents. Illusioning, fantasizing or blocking out might be used. Unfortunately for the present time adult, they are unaware of these trances, while the observer remains fast asleep. In another scenario, the inner child within the adult makes his spouse into an ideal by "building her up," making the spouse feel good about herself. In this case, the child within believes, "If I build you up, you'll take care of me." To be taken care of is a normal wish. Unfortunately, in a dysfunctional family, this is a desperate wish because care and love are unavailable.

Adult Problem State: Idealizing other people, lessening yourself in order to idealize others. In this case the child within who is idealizing gives up her own power or, worse yet, pretends she doesn't have any. This child-like position gives others power and claims none for itself.

Women and Power

...we insult them everyday on T.V.
...and wonder why they have no guts or confidence
...when they are young we kill their will to be free
...by telling them not to be smart and then put them down for being dumb.

"Women Are the Nigger's of the World"
John Lennon
inspired by Yoko Ono

In our male dominated society, often the little girl inside a woman plays dumb, or hides her power. The little girl knows how fragile a man's ego is, so she builds him up as an ideal. This makes her and him feel more secure. This trance keeps her relationship but at the price of hiding her own power and brilliance. In many cases she pretends she's not as smart as he, to the point she forgets she is pretending. Many times, mothers teach their daughters to not be powerful. Since, in our society this is taught and re-enforced, the inner child within a woman hides its power. In workshop after workshop, women are continually presenting the problem of re-pressed power. Interestingly, very often the mother teaches and is the model for repressing ones personal power. An example in recent years is the Equal Rights Amendment (ERA). This amendment guarantees equal rights to women. What is astonishing is that the little girl inside the adult woman has been so trained to hide her power and has pretended so long that she is less than a man, that she has forgotten she is pretending. Thus, many *conservative* women demonstrate their age regression by being against their own equal rights!

> *Adult Problem States:* The next major problem arises when disappointments come from the spouse not matching the idealizations. In this style, the child within the man tries to make his spouse into an ideal. Frustration escalates since nobody can equal someone else's internal ideal. This idealization trance also prevents the man from dealing with his reality and relationship *now*.

In these situations there are two trances which occur.

1. The child idealizes Mom and Dad to survive.
2. The child within the adult generalizes this strategy to his spouse, illusioning them to be something they are not, to continue the childhood trance.

In these two trances, the inner child (1) defends himself from who the person truly is, and (2) trance-fers this defensive style on his spouse making them his ideal, thus protecting the old reality and avoiding the new reality.

In most cases, the trance of idealization is a powerful defense the child uses to help her survive. The idealization trance enables the child to not feel, see, or even recognize the pain in her dysfunctional family.

Spiritualization
The Third Level Processes

Spiritualizing is the third level trance. It is an outgrowth of levels one and two. In order to spiritualize, an individual must go through the first two levels. Spiritualization is very deep, rooted in pre-verbal cognition and deeply involves survival. Spiritualizing is difficult to spot within oneself because books, philosophies, and "spiritual groups" help to validate the trance and continue to hypnotize the infant within the adult. It should be noted that not everyone goes through the trance of spiritualization. If an individual developmentally does not complete and pass through process one and the second process completely, they will stumble into the third process of spiritualization. To explain further, most children will idealize their parents. Eventually, people realize that their parents are just people, with good and bad qualities. This would end the second process of idealizing, and the person would probably not spiritualize. If, however, the infant within the adult still has this developmental gap and is, hence, developmentally delayed, and they continue idealizing others—they will enter the third process of spiritualization of SUPER-IDEALIZING.

Below are the types, problem states, and trances of spiritualization.

The Infant Trance

In the third level of spiritualization, the adult is hypnotized by the infant's magical thinking. This becomes a major cognition for people who get involved with magic, and who think they can create or influence others. For example in workshops I am asked "Don't you think thoughts create reality?" To meet this level of magical thinking or grandiosity disguised in a spiritual philosophy, I ask the group, "How many people have you thought about having sex with?" I let them think about that. "Now, how many people have you had sex with? Notice the discrepancy. If thought creates reality, it's a poor means of creation."

Transpersonal Trance-ference

Transpersonal *trance*-ference is a process by which an infant imagines his parents as God. The infant believes his parents are all-good, all-powerful, all-loving and all-knowing. This is re-enforced by parents that suggest this is true. For example, a little girl has to play Dad's game in order to survive. In order not to feel the pain of giving up oneself to survive, the *observer* creates the idea within the infant that Dad is a god-like figure.

A possible outcome is, years later the infant within the adult is attracted to and joins a "spiritual group." This group has a philosophy and rules for getting God's Love (which is really Dad's and Mom's love), or rules for getting to heaven, winning grace, getting liberation, bliss, etc. It is the infant within the adult who is drawn into this *famil*-iar game of the family. Simply put, the infant within feels overwhelmingly connected and attracted to spiritual groups and philosophies that mirror her family of origin. This attraction to such groups, communities or philosophies is because they are family replicas from the past. This is the spiritualization process.

The trance-fer of the parent to idealized parent to the God who grants grace by giving rewards, or a fall from the parental/God path or grace and receiving punishments, is a process the child frequently goes through. From the infant's point of view, it is by the power of parents/Gods that the child came to earth. Why? Because to an infant, his whole universe, life and death are dependent upon parents/God. The infant/child remains frozen within the adult seeking "the answer," or ways to get to heaven, peace or liberation. Often this is trance-fered to a teacher or guide who gives the answer to the question, "how do I get free?" Transpersonal trance-ference onto guides or teachers who have the answers, similar to parents, runs parallel. For example, many clients I have worked with look for their purpose or the meaning of life, seeking teacher after teacher for that "higher purpose." The problem is that the infant/child within is running the show. The infant/child within the adult is the seeker. This is a very age-regressed, and pre-verbal trance, which requires the looking to another for power, love, or enlightenment, rather than to *oneself*. The solidity of this state is strong, because it was formed preverbally by an infant who had to look to another for the secret of survival. Parents determine the most basic life and death issues of the child: the maintenance of the physical body and ultimate well-being. Unfortunately for many, that infantile state stays frozen long after it has developmentally served its purpose.

Adult Problem State: Super-Idealizing people. They are God. If I do what they say, I won't get punished (fall off the path), and I'll attain nirvana, heaven, etc. My nirvana was house, job and kids. This was my father's path to nirvana. Super-idealizing is the trance-fer of God-like qualities onto people, making people into gurus, and asking them for help as if they had the power to grant your wishes or fulfill your dreams. The *magical thinking* of first level development is trance-ferred onto a person, "as if" their thoughts had the power to awaken you. The child transfers his grandiosity onto a person, making him, as he did to his parents, into a saint, guru, etc. This infantile state is reinforced by philosophies like the guru system of Hinduism, or the Roman Catholic system of the Pope, i.e., the intermediary between people and God. This trance creates religious systems and volumes of books of study, which *reinforce the truth of the system.*

Spiritualization Commandment: do unto a person, that which you did unto yourself with your parents, in order to survive. In other words, make people into gods.

Trance-ferring onto a System

In this infant/child-like trance of spiritualization, an infant/child transfers the past idealization onto a spiritual system. In spiritual systems, the infant/child within the adult overlays her system on the world. This makes the world a "play of God," (a play of Mom/Dad), or a way to learn lessons (Mom's/Dad's lessons). This child within the system gives its power away to "a higher power." The *tautology* is that the adult relates only to the child within, transferring its world onto the confused world of Mom and Dad and then making it spiritual. This offers the adult, currently being hypnotized by the infant/child, no feedback loop with the world.

In the same way, religious systems relate to themselves with no feedback from the world. The religious system becomes a *tautology* because it never looks outside of itself for answers; it only looks at itself or within its system for the answers. When the system cannot find an answer, or shall I say when Dad/Mom don't have the answer, the child or system employ super-spiritualization, such as "God works in mysterious ways." The parents who have been made into gods *do* act in mysterious ways, particularly if they are *alcoholic*. This parallels the rationalization of the child within the adult when teachers or gurus "act crazy." Some systems even call this "crazy wisdom." This keeps the religious or spiritual system, which is really the family, alive. This philosophy is portrayed in the book the *Peter Principle*. Peter's second principle, "At all costs the hierarchy must be preserved," which is similar to the spiritual hierarchy and family hierarchy which preserves itself at all costs. For example, look at the lengths the Catholic Church has gone through to *preserve the hierarchy*, even in the face of the sexual abuse of children!

Adult Problem State: Transparency. Problem states continue to occur as the child within *trance*-fers his spiritualizing onto others. For example, the child imagines himself to be transparent and that the idealized guru/parent can see his every thought, or knows his real self. This is grandiosity in reverse. Here the child idealizes and *trance*-fers grandiose powers on another figure, making the person a superhuman God/guru, thus making the figure grandiose.

Trance-fer of Values and Lessons

In other forms of transpersonal transference, the child trance-fers parental values to God. Here the child develops the trance of transferring to God his parents' good/bad system, which the child has taken on to survive. Now, good actions (the ones Dad and Mom like) are what God wants. Bad actions become what God doesn't want. Parental punishment occurs when a child doesn't get something from her parents. The parent says, "You're not getting this to learn a lesson." Years later, when the adult doesn't get something in life she wants, the infant/child within the adult uses spiritual reframes like, "God is trying to teach me a lesson."

Trance-fer into a Spiritual Path

In another trance style, the child *trance*-fers the parent's way of being into a spiritual path. The child is given a path, a means or is told how to get to a particular end point. For example a middle class scenario would be the good boy following Dad's path, such as college, graduate school, marriage, three kids, and a house in suburbia. This is viewed through the eyes of the infant/child as "the word of God." Years later, the path or "how to" is generalized into something spiritual applying to life, enlightenment, liberation or knowing God. Parent/Gods gave the child the message, "This is the best, only, highest or fastest" way to a house in the suburbs" (liberation or God). The child within the adult becomes rigid, and fanatic. In Eric Hoffa's book, *"The True Believer,"* he states that the same rigid structure that governs Nazis also governs religious fanatics, although the goals are different.

> *Adult Problem State:* Spiritualization and Rationalization. If I need it my parents/God will give it to me. If I don't need it, I won't get it. I would say to my parents, "I want a new bike." My parents would say, "You don't need a new bike; if you needed it, we would give it to you." this is interpreted by the infant/child as God gives me what I need, with the spiritualization that when something doesn't come that you want, "I guess God didn't want me to have it, or "I guess I didn't need it." Notice how the infant/child within the adult spiritualizes that God decided I didn't need it. It's as if God said, "Give Stephen money, he needs it," or "Don't give him money; he needs to learn a lesson."

Transpersonal Co-dependence

In this third level process, the child pleases and serves the parents in order to get taken care of. Psychologically, the child inside a woman might believe "I'll take care of you (help you through medical school), so that you'll take care of me." This is a story of a child who gives up her self to take care of her parents in order to be taken care of herself. A child brought up in an alcoholic family might clean-up Dad's bottle of booze, thinking that's taking care of him so that she will be taken care of.

Years later, if it *trance*-fers to God (transpersonal co-dependence), the child within might become a disciple of a guru. The philosophies match: I'll serve the guru, so he will take care of me. Notice how often gurus and religious systems abuse their vulnerable disciples sexuality and emotionally. It appears to the child within the disciple that he is serving, but actually the guru is manipulating, playing out the parent side of the identity, getting people to take care of him in the name of spirituality. This is called service. People in spiritual circles say things like, "I just want to serve God." Translated, "I want to take care of Mom and Dad, so I will get taken care of."

Notice how the trance of spiritualization organizes the chaos of being brought up in a dysfunctional family, giving it to a higher and more dissociated purpose. In the song, *Do You Remember*, John Lennon says, "Do you remember when you were small. How people seemed so tall?" This is the higher power phenomenon. The child has to *look up* to parents because children are physically smaller and less developed. Notice in most religions, you "look up" to God; this is the child's re-creation of being small, looking up at parents now called "God." This pre-supposes God has a location.* This ordering of chaos by the child is a powerful way he can avoid his personal pain and be grandiose about his own specialness.

The illusion of the child within is that she is serving some higher person, so that the "higher person" will take care of her by giving her knowledge, love, etc. The child is physically smaller and sees adults as bigger, thus attributing higher knowledge, and in many cases magical power, which are spiritualized parents.

Adult Problem State: Parallel spiritual systems. Spiritual systems match psychological distortions, and the child within will be attracted to spiritual systems that re-enforce his first level, second level, and third level cognitions.

Adult Problem State: Projection of God on a loved one. "That person is my only source of love, affection, etc." The child imagines that parents are their *only source* of love *forever*. A child that has not owned his own self love, imagines that love is something given or taken away and that he is not the source of his own love. Psychologically, it is easy to see how the child within, who is a "love addict," could transfer onto a person the label *only source of love*. Spiritually, however, parents and gurus become the only

---

* See *Quantum Consciousness: The Guide to Experiencing Quantum Psychology* by Stephen Wolinsky, 1993, Bramble Books. Bell's Theorem is discussed regarding no locality.

source of love, and the addiction gets fixated on something outside of themselves. Notice in how many spiritual groups you have to win the love or grace of the guru, to attain what you want (enlightenment or a bicycle). This is similar to the child's relationship to his parents. This trance of the inner child (making someone the source of your love) steals the responsibility of the adult who now believes someone else is responsible for his love of self or how he feels about himself. *You are responsible for your perception and your experience of love or lack of love*.

Adult Problem State: The guru (parent) is responsible for my spiritual growth. In this scenario the child feels, and rightly so, that his growth both physically and psychologically, is dependent on his parents. The parents are responsible for feeding and otherwise taking care of their children. Children are vulnerable and need their parents' care. Hence, they are dependent and powerless. When the person separates from the parents, then their child "grows up," taking responsibility for her own physical and psychological growth and well-being. If, however, the child stays *fixated*, the child within the adult *trance*-fers this desire to be taken care of onto a guru/God, who becomes responsible for her spiritual growth. In one community in India, the teaching was, "The guru takes responsibility for your spiritual unfolding." Notice how the inner child within the adult will be attracted to philosophies that keep the trance alive and well. We must understand that the path *feels right* to the inner child, because it is *famil*-iar, similar to the family/ child trance.

Adult Problem State: Family and spiritual rejection. In every spiritual group, I have encountered people who feel finished or who aren't following the path (game) any longer. They are harassed by the other family/spiritual members. When a child leaves home in a dysfunctional family, the parents and other family members send the message, "There's something wrong with that boy/girl," or, "They are doing it the wrong way and will fail." It is an interesting parallel in spiritual groups. When a member wants to leave—outgrows the group or feels finished—the group says, "He/she *fell* from the path, didn't really *surrender*, was *resisting*, or had some *worldly stuff* to work out." The spiritualization of the dysfunctional family parallels the spiritual group.

Adult Problem State: I am entitled. This concept comes from the child who believes, and arguably so, that he is entitled to be taken care of just because of who he is. This is a normal phase of development that, when interrupted, keeps the person stuck at this child-like level of "the world owes me a living."

Spiritualizing pain

Another third level process is spiritualizing pain. In the spiritualization trance, lessons to be learned seem to be the common explanation for pain. While living in a monastery in India, often we would get letters from the West saying something like, "I'm really learning a lot," "I'm really growing a lot," or "I've learned a lot of lessons about life," and we would laugh and say to each other, "Boy, they must really be in pain." This form of *spiritual reframe* has become popular lately. Some might argue it has value in presenting people with a different perspective on their situation. This may be true, but the issue of pain, chaos, and the case of spiritual reframing to organize it, comes into question.

Societal Spiritual Trances: Karma Theory

Karma is the Asian concept, "What you sow, so shall you reap." Consider how this concept developed in India and how it helps to organize the chaos and keeps order in the society. In India more than 99% of the wealth is owned by less than 1% of the population. Karma theory helps to organize the pain and chaos of the 99%. Furthermore, we must look at the larger context of religious and spiritual systems to appreciate their attempt to organize the chaos. For example, in India you develop the karma theory, (i.e., I have less in this life because of my deeds in another life. If I'm *good* in this life, I'll get *good* in future lives.) The karma theory prevents the chaos of the poor 99% from overthrowing the rich 1%. How else but using spiritualization, God, and karma theory could the masses be controlled? In short, Karma theory is a spiritual philosophy used to explain and maintain the economic status of Asia.

Karma Theory Spiritualizations:
"It is my Karma from my past life that I'm balancing; that's why I'm in pain" (I didn't get what I wanted). Here, in order for the child to find a way to make sense out of a need unfulfilled, she *trance*-fers a system to organize the discomfort and chaos. Children do not understand why their needs are not being fulfilled. This is re-enforced *culturally* in Asia and, in Western cultures, by spiritualization. It is an opiate to dull the frustration and chaos that might cause people to demand their rights and make a change. Below is another form of spiritualizing pain I call super trance-personal spiritualizations.

Review of Super Trance-personal Spiritualization Rationalizations

1. When you don't get what you want, "God/parents has other things in mind for me, higher purposes."

2. When things seem chaotic, "God works in mysterious ways."

3. When you're good and don't get rewarded, "I will get my reward for being good in another life," or "They will get their punishment in another life, for being bad now."

In cognitive therapy this thinking distortion is called, Heaven's Reward Fallacy.

"In this framework for viewing the world, you always do the "right thing" in hope of reward. You sacrifice and slave, and all the while imagine you are collecting "brownie points" you can cash in some day. (McKay, 1981:25)

Notice how rooted this is in the infant or inner child state. In the spiritualizing process, this is a constant occurrence. An example is the Hindu systems of work and sacrifice for liberation. In the

Christian religion, sacrifice is seen as noble. The problem is that all to often people sacrifice themselves with hope of being rewarded, and the reward doesn't come. The infant/child within reduces the world to simple units of cause (I'm good) yields effect (I get money, power, God, etc.).

4. *Specialness*. Specialness is a third level trance the child creates in which they see themselves as special, as a *reaction formation* or defense for not getting the caretaking they imagine they are entitled to. Years later the child within the adult expects to be taken care of for being good, or just *special*. The child cannot process the chaos of neglect or abuse and so decides there must be a purpose, and as a reaction creates specialness. *Specialness* is a process in which the child creates a feeling of being special or different from others rather than dealing with her neglect or abuse. The defense of specialness is re-enforced by slogans like, "You're special."

Recall on the television comedy show *Saturday Night Live*, the Church Lady, in a sarcastic voice always said two things; "Well, isn't that special," and "feeling just a little bit superior." Notice how people on spiritual paths feel special, or chosen, or superior to everyone else.

Recently at a workshop, a participant asked, "How do I know if I'm in the inner child identity?" I responded, "When you feel special or different from others, you are in an identity." A few years ago a well known therapist asked me, "Suppose I like feeling special?" I responded by saying, "With the identity of feeling special comes the feelings of separation, disconnection, feeling like nobody understands, loneliness, alienation, and possibly depression. This is not a small price to pay for the inner child's desire to defend against chaos by creating the feeling of being special."

Specialness and spiritualizing defend the child from the chaos he/she would have to face being raised in a dysfunctional family. Often times "incest survivors" feel special because they were "chosen" by Dad/Mom to receive this *special* attention. This child-like internal trance leaves an adult feeling:

Misunderstood—"Don't people see I'm special?"
Alienated—"I have a secret (the incest) that would blow people away and hence nobody understands me, or
Unseen—People don't see my depth or people don't see me.

Spiritualizing and Specializing

In this spiritualizing trance of specialness, the secret (incest) is hidden from the child. The parents, who are now unconsciously seen as gods, have the secret. Later in life the child within the adult might be attracted to a guru who implies, "I have the secret. The inner child within the adult feels compelled to find out, or know the truth, in the belief that "The truth will set you free." In that way the inner child is compulsively drawn to a guru who claims to know the truth and will, since she is *special*, impart this secret to her. In my circumstance, it was the truth of my incest that set me free from the trance of spiritualizing. In my case I went to gurus to help me find the secret that was hidden from me, and which the inner child had hidden from me. I had transferred my parents on the guru, who I imagined knew the "secret." The guru exhibits *counter-trance-ference*. He represents the other side of the identity, pretending either he knows the secret of freedom, or claims he is free and, therefore, can unlock the hidden secret within you. Often the guru suggests methods or ways to unlock these secrets of the universe. Here the guru believes he has the way, and the child within the adult *trance*-fers his parents onto the guru, in hope of finding the way out of the maze of the secret, (i.e. the incest or dysfunction.) The secret is spiritualized, being called "maya" (the illusion) in some Asian systems. The Guru did not know the secret of my incest. I spiritualized the secret, and him, believing the truth will set me free. In this case the *truth of my incest set me free of the spiritualizing trance*.

Spiritualized Abuse

In all too many cases gurus and teachers emotionally or sexually abuse their students and disciples. Unfortunately, since to the inner child within the adult this is familiar, it is accepted, denied or spiritualized. In one case, an Indian guru would preach being celibate, while sleeping with underage disciples. This was spiritualized by other abused disciples as Tantra, (a secret sexual yoga of liberation). In another case, the teacher suggested everybody sleep with everybody and spiritualized it with, "You must keep having sex until it is unimportant." A third teacher slept with his disciples and denied it. It is interesting that the inner child of the teacher also denied it publicly. This is because the degree to which the teacher/guru/parent denies his drinking or abuse, equals the degree to which the denial exists within the child inside of the disciple. One teacher, died of cirrhosis of the liver and was a known alcoholic. To handle this chaotic discrepancy the inner child within his students spiritualized it saying, "He drank and had sex for us, to teach us he was human."

Unfortunately the gurus and teachers are as involved in spiritualizing as the disciples, hence the attraction (like attracts like). This duplicates the process with the parents. The victim-abuser or disciple-guru are two sides of the inner child identity trance.

The Inner Children within the Guru

Let me state this more clearly. The guru has two inner spiritualized children. One has fused with the grandiosity, and one is the unknowing child. The disciple has the same two inner children. The disciple *trance*-fers the all-knowing grandiosity on the guru, making him into an all-knowing saint. The guru *counter-trance*-fers this, becoming the grandiose teacher. The guru *trance*-fers his unknowing inner child on the disciple and then the disciple is seen as unknowing and ignorant. The *trance*-ference must be broken and dismantled for the observer to wake-up and true inner awareness to develop. Unfortunately, all too often the guru or therapist gets addicted to the adulation of the disciple, and becomes blinded by his/her own *trance*-ference and *counter-trance*-ference issues. To explain further, I recently spent time visiting a therapy guru. One of his disciples, a woman about 50, came over to him, acting about age 5, clearly treating him as Daddy. Instead of breaking her *trance*-ference, he liked the adulation and became the all-wise therapy guru. Although this felt comfortable to both of them, it was familiar (as in family), keeping the disciple and the therapy guru age-regressed. For myself when my incest was uncovered and handled, my spiritualizing ended.

What makes this style so interesting is the rage, implicit demands, and the internal manipulations this inner child will go through in order to be taken care of and to rationalize the abuse by a teacher, and how the teacher can justify her mistreatment in terms of spirituality.

Gurus and Teachers Breaking-Up Marriages

Many disciples and students of teachers have often times had their marriages or relationships broken-up or certainly interfered with by Gurus or teachers. Why?

In this scenario the Guru is acting out his/her *Oedipus* complex.

Oedipus Complex: The unresolved desire of the child for sexual gratification through the parent of the opposite sex. This involves first, identification with and, later, hatred for the parent of the same sex, who is considered by the child as a rival. (American College Dictionary, pg. 840)

How does this apply? A married couple comes to a Guru and age-regresses and spiritualizes the Guru/Dad, next, the Guru age-regresses and makes the married couple into *his* mom and dad. Next, the age-regressed Guru, does what he can to inter-*fear* with the couple, so he can have the woman, (Mom) for himself.

In India, this used to be called left-handed *shaktipat*. *Shaktipat* is a term used to describe initiation by a Guru. In left-handed *shaktipat,* the Guru initiates the husband and wife, and then tries to, or sleeps with the wife.

This age-regression by the guru and age-regression and spiritualization by the disciples, has done great damage to both individuals and couples. Unfortunately this occurs, and even more unfortunately, the Guru's behavior is spiritualized rather than being confronted and seen as the age-regressed trance of a perpetrator.

The Spiritual Lesson Reframe and Trance

As children we are all given reasons why things occur. Generally speaking parents give a reason for rewards or punishments. For example, a child who does what is suggested by Mom and Dad gets rewarded, now or in the future. Children who don't do what parents tell them are punished now or in the future. If our previous discussion is correct, and we make our parents into gods who are trying to teach us lessons, let us look at the possible outcomes.

A child is rewarded for learning the lesson of cleaning his room. Another child is punished by parents for not learning the lesson. When the child is asked, "Why am I being punished?" parents say, because you need to learn lessons.

Years later in school, a similar model of rewards and punishments is fused with the concept of lessons. For example if I learn my arithmetic lesson, I'm rewarded. If I don't, I'm punished (have to do extra homework). What impact could occur in the future. "If I am good, God gives me more things" (bliss, money, good relationship, etc.) because I learned my lesson. If something bad happens, I must have a lesson to learn. Spiritualization believes in Good behavior = Good outcomes, Bad behavior = bad outcomes. If I'm good I'll get; if I'm bad I won't get. Good people get good, bad people get bad. Chaos occurs because this is not the case.

The Discrepancy

For example, Mafia people own houses on the beach, and good people get stuck with bad cars. Incongruent experience causes chaos, to be rationalized spiritually by the child within. "I guess the person had karma from another life. That's why good didn't happen to a good person." Or, "I wonder what lessons they need to learn?" "I wonder why they created bad happenings to themselves."

Spiritual Reframes and Rationalizations

1. Bad happens to Good: "I guess that there is a lesson they needed to learn."
2. Bad happens to Good: "There must be a higher purpose or higher plan."
3. God gives me what I need: "When you don't get what you need, you must not have really needed it."

Spiritualization has very strong cultural roots. Schools of thought, philosophies, which give ways to alleviate suffering, are deeply rooted in the inner child. What is the central issue? Organizing chaos.

For some reason, possibly due to the cause-effect and linear nature of thoughts, we resist chaos. Noted Feldenkrais trainer Dr. Carl Ginsburg related a story to me about the founder of Feldenkrais (a form of body-mind awareness), Moshe Feldenkrais. Feldenkrais was leading a training and asked the group of about 60 trainees, "What is the purpose of the nervous system?"

Students came up with all sorts of answers which Feldenkrais dismissed. His answer? "The purpose of the nervous system is to organize chaos."

In the same way, the inner child organizes chaos by transferring the system she created to handle Mom and Dad onto the rest of the world. The child inside the adult can roll along on automatic pilot, treating the past as the present, creating the future from the memory of the past, in an attempt to fit the present-time world into a system that appears to make sense. Problems arise for the adult because the child within does not let in information contrary to the system, thus freezing the child within the adult. The world becomes familiar and stable but rigid, boring and robotic. It is the resistance to chaos emptiness or unexplainability of life that creates systems that organize chaos, and keep age-regressed inner children creating worlds that limit ours and others' freedom.

5. *Inner World Trances of the Dark Side of the Inner Child: Gods and Goddesses.* For those of us who were unable to idealize parents or make them into gods, comes a different third level trance state, an **internalized**, idealized Mom/Dad and the inner-God trance. For example in the case of a wounded child who cannot idealize his external mother as "all-powerful," "all- good," or "all-knowing" comes a new and improved trance: creating an inner world. Idealized Moms/Dads become "inner gods," or "inner goddesses." In Eastern cultures, worship of the inner mother, goddess or Devi is prescribed to handle the ills of life. Certainly most religious systems ask you to find the God within. This is a brilliant way to handle the external chaos of a dysfunctional family. Create an inner-idealized family and then spiritualize them. A child cannot depend on the outer Mom or Dad, so why not create an idealized inner Mom and Dad? Then through transpersonal transference, which resists chaos, have the created internal gods and goddesses give us the answers and explanations the other Dad/gods and Mom/goddesses could not. Often archetypes are internalized, idealized moms and dads that the child created because there was no one to fulfill these roles.

In some psychologies and religious systems, the inner is said to be better than the outer. Inner gods/goddesses are better (more ideal), and people who are introverted are more evolved than those who are extroverted. When a system is created to make sense of the world and the world makes no sense to the inner child, developing an introverted system with *super*-idealized parents (now called gods or goddesses), keeps the psychological system of the inner child alive.

Lies

At this juncture I wish to reiterate the same point made in the preamble. It is not my desire to destroy, blame, or shame those involved in a spiritual group or system. The emphasis on a spiritual group, however, could be better served by each individual taking responsibility for his trances. Stated another way, P.D. Ouspensky, noted Fourth Way teacher, called psychology the study of *lies*. Each one of us is responsible for the lies he/she erects and tells to herself. A true spiritual warrior needs to look at, acknowledge and dismantle these lies. This takes great courage. It is not for me to say whether or not you are lying to yourself and spiritualizing; that is your job. I am attempting to point out possible pitfalls that I have observed within myself.

Recently workshop participants asked me why there was such a lack of integrity in the world. I said, "Lies and integrity are not black or white. Integrity begins inside oneself, not outside oneself. The more you lie to yourself, the more you lie to others."

In the ancient yoga system, called Raja Yoga, the first preliminary steps ask the participant to not lie. This is really about not telling lies to yourself to avoid pain. Therefore, it is the purpose of this section to uncover at all costs the lies you tell yourself, no matter how small. Therein is freedom.

An incest survivor from a dysfunctional family experiences chaos. He is driven to create a good Dad inside, who is always there, calm and peaceful. This gives the child's life meaning and stability, but it robs the individual of understanding. By creating structures (lies) to handle chaos, we lose ourselves: the one who is observing and creating these structures. To give another example of the self-to-self lie, recently I was giving a workshop in the Midwest. The man sponsoring me was complaining about a woman with whom he was involved. He said, "I can't believe I chose the same type of woman again." I said, "That's because you lied to yourself from the beginning." After a moment or two of shock he said, "You know, you're right. I knew from the beginning what was happening, and lied to myself." This freed him immensely, because he could now *take responsibility* for his actions rather than feeling victimized by her actions.

In my case, the most powerful feeling of interconnection and unity with humanity I ever experienced was at my first Incest

Survivors Anonymous Group. Why? Because the lies I told myself and the pretending I played with others, in a moment of telling the truth, disappeared. It takes an immense amount of energy to hold back a secret and lie and pretend. When those lies are admitted as lies, the vulnerability and interconnection naturally occurs. This is the key point to remember. If our ultimate goal is to discover *who we are*, then the most important step is to look at our created internal realities, acknowledging their purpose, studying how they help us to resist or organize chaos. The final step is to discover ourselves as the observer and the creator of our internal images and experiences. This allows us to face ourselves more directly, and finally to break through beyond even the observer and the reality created by the observer. This is discussed and explored in detail in an experiential way in my book *Quantum Consciousness: The Guide to Experiencing Quantum Psychology*.

The Nervous System

Many forms of psychotherapy suggest integrating or getting in touch with your inner gods or goddesses. This phenomenon, according to Carl Jung, M.D., appears in a similar way in Eastern, Western as well as rich/poor, primitive and industrialized societies. This way of handling chaos, what Jung calls an "archtype," might be the universal way that the nervous system organizes chaos. This understanding de-mystifies the world of the collective unconscious. Might not the internal creation be a wish or attempt to create an understanding to avoid chaos? In India praying to the Divine Mother is culturally acceptable as is praying to Mother Mary for Roman Catholics. Possibly, the collective unconscious is not where these universal experiences live, but rather are a collective defensive trance structure, which is cross-cultural and universal, a part of the nervous system developed to organize the pain and chaos of life.

If this be the case, then we may not be subject to a mystical world of gods and goddesses but rather a world of created gods and goddess, created by the child and passed down from generation to generation in the form of ritual, tradition and folklore.*

It is not my goal to destroy belief structures. It is my purpose to *empower you, the creator of the belief structure*. When finding out

---

*This topic will be discussed in detail in a forthcoming book, *The Tao of Chaos: Quantum Consciousness* Vol. II: by the same author.

who you are, all belief structures, that are like *sacred cows*, stand in the way! Noted philosopher Alfred Korsybski said, "The map, is not the territory." In this way beliefs, ideas, images are not you. Rather you are the observer and creator (the territory) of the images (the map).

The Next Step
Handling Spiritualization

1. Notice what religious or spiritual philosophy your inner child seems to be attracted to.
2. Write down the basic beliefs of that spiritual or religious philosophy.
3. Notice the beliefs of the inner child and write them down. Note that the beliefs of the inner infant, (being taken care of) are often "wishes."
4. Compare the two belief structures to see if there is a parallel.
5. Notice where the inner child may live in your body (mouth, heart, pelvis, etc.).
6. Notice which spiritualization trances you're inner infant/child uses. If many spiritual beliefs match the beliefs of the inner child, then identify which ones fit from the list below.

   a. *Trance*-personal *trance*-ference:
   b. *Trance-personal Co-dependence*
   c. Specializing Pain
   d. Specializing
   e. Internal Gods and Goddesses

2. Identify the spiritualizations, generalizations, and beliefs the inner child has and write them down.
3. Identify the spiritual or psychological philosophy that the inner child belongs to or believes as true.
4. Dialogue with the inner child asking questions and writing down the inner child's answers.

a. What do you (the inner child) not know about yourself?

b. What do you (the inner child) resist?

c. By you (the inner child) taking on and believing a philosophy, what are you avoiding experiencing?

d. By you (the inner child) taking on this philosophy are you resisting chaos?

e. By you (the inner child) taking on this philosophy are you resisting the unknown?

f. By you (the inner child) taking on this philosophy are you resisting confusion?

g. By you (the inner child) taking on this philosophy are you resisting being overwhelmed?

h. By you (the inner child) taking on this philosophy are you resisting fear?

i. By you (the inner child) taking on this philosophy are you resisting loss of self?

j. By you (the inner child) taking on this philosophy are you resisting being out of control?

k. By you (the inner child) taking on this philosophy are you resisting emptiness?

l. By you (the inner child) taking on this philosophy are you resisting feeling crazy?

m. By you (the inner child) taking on this philosophy are you resisting the void?

n. By you (the inner child) taking on this philosophy are you resisting space?

o. When did you (the inner child) decide to take on a spiritual or psychological system to handle one or more of the above? Write down your answers.

p. Is there an incident, trauma, or event that you (the inner child) witnessed or observed which solidified the system or world view? Write down your answer.

q. Ask yourself: If I give up the inner child's spiritualization, what would be left? Write down your answer.

r. Noting what would be left, ask yourself: Am I willing to give up the inner child's trance of spiritualizing? If not, why not?

s. If no, ask yourself: What am I resisting by not giving up the spiritualization? Write down your answer.

Homework

Part 1. For this week, every time a spiritualization or method of organizing chaos comes into your mind, call it out and label it "spiritualization trance."

Part 2. Note how spiritualization helps to explain the unexplainable in life.

Conclusion

This format provides a step that will get you more in touch with the different spiritualizations that occur. This provides an ability to observe and interrupt the pop-up ideas of life, which get in the way of experiencing life in the present. Earlier I mentioned awareness as the solvent to the glue of spiritualization. Spiritualization is a two-edged sword. Although it provides temporary comfort from chaos, it robs you in *present time* of a world view without past inter-*fear*-ence. The intention is to free you from past-world views of the inner child/infant. The child within has a window that it looks through. This view when left behind offers us the opportunity to enjoy present-time experience and the freedom of pure, uninterrupted awareness, uninhibited by memory, distortion, or resistance to chaos. It is in this pure, uninterrupted awareness and self-remembering, without past inter-*fear*-ence, that the natural interconnection and unity becomes available. This natural unity consciousness, called "quantum consciousness," is the force and connection that provides us with true, natural, effortless spirituality. This is our birthright, and this becomes an experiential knowingness, as the past and automatic trance associations of the inner-child are *trance-ended.*

> *When I was a child,*
> *I spoke as a child,*
> *I understood as a child,*
> *I thought as a child:*
> *But when I became an adult, I put away childish things.*

The Bible
1 Corinthians, 13:11

•Epilogue

Foundations of Identities, The Tao of Chaos

As we say good bye for now to the inner child identity, what are we saying hello to? To begin with, the inner child identity, with all its trances, strategies, thoughts, and feelings, was born of two parents, *chaos and resistance*. If Moshe Feldenkrais is right that the purpose of the nervous system is to organize chaos, then the observer uses the inner child to organize chaos by creating strategies to deal with dysfunctional family life. This inner child, is a manifestation of the observer and the creative aspect of our nervous system.

Although the inner child helped our survival by deadening—or certainly dampening—sensory input, that deadening robbed us of our true nature. Truly, few of us could deny that a child born of chaos and resistance to chaos can do little but create more chaos in its internal subjective world and the external world. As we say good-bye to this child of chaos, it is important to open a new chapter working with, absorbing, and living in chaos without re-creating it automatically. My forthcoming book, *The Tao of Chaos:* Essence and the Enneagram, Quantum Consciousness, Volume II was written with this agenda in mind.

As you recall from an earlier section of this book, chaos was defined by as

"utter confusion or disorder, wholly without organization or order." (American College Dictionary, pg. 20)

Certainly we have seen that the inner child is a manifestation of that disorder or, in psychological terms, dysfunction.

The second definition of chaos by Webster,

"the infinity of space or formless matter supposed to have preceded the existence of the ordered universe," (American College Dictionary, pg. 201)

will take the front seat in *The Tao of Chaos.* Why do we all resist nothingness or what the Buddhist calls "void"? Let me explain by calling to mind two people who came to see me for psychotherapy.

The first person, a businessman, suffered from acute anxiety. We first took apart the trances and the basic structures of his inner child. What was left was a much deeper, much more terrifying and much more resisted experience... the feeling of *void*, no-thing-ness. We found that this man had resisted this ever-present void within himself to so intense a degree because he felt he would be swallowed up by it and disappear.

Since chaos also is defined as the "infinity of space," our work began to move in the direction of seeing the void as a friend, always there, untouched and quiet. His anxiety disappeared. Why? He no longer was resisting that void or chaos.

Another example was a woman medical doctor who came to see me, suffering from obsessive-compulsive thoughts and behavior. This included everything from work to relationships. She sought my help because after having left her home at 19 to get married, and a divorce after 25 years of marriage, she had gotten immediately into another relationship. Now as this new relationship of four years was ending, she was in terror. Once again we processed through the identities and strategies of the past and present, but the terror still remained. Once again, I was struck by her resistance to the emptiness, which she felt was always there as a threat. Her obsessive-compulsive tendency was a way to resist the void by trying to *fill it up*. We worked through the impossibility of filling up the void, and as she began allowing the emptiness rather than resisting it, the terror subsided. She felt calm and at peace. Furthermore, in addition to the terror leaving and the obsessive-compulsive attempts to fill up the emptiness leaving, her fear of being alone, which was associated with the emptiness, also departed.

Looking at the inner emptiness represents the more sedate side of what would normally be called chaos and became my own next stage of development. I explored the newly emerging "theory of chaos," born of physics, and its application to the field of psychology and self help. My upcoming book is about looking at chaos as it reflects our daily problems and solutions, hence its title, *The Tao of Chaos*. *Tao* is the Chinese term for "The Way," or the way of chaos.

In this book, along with my earlier works, *Trances People Live: Healing Approaches in Quantum Psychology*, and *Quantum Consciousness: The Guide to Experiencing Quantum Psychology*, we looked at identities, roles, trances and their relationships to psychology, physics, and religions.

The Tao of Chaos will provide methods and approaches to embrace chaos and its sister, the void, as means to discovering a deeper sense of who we are without resistance.

With love,
your brother
Stephen

•Appendix I

The Trigger, Changing the Button

A "trigger" is a button that gets pushed and that begins the uncomfortable emergence of a problem state. Most of us are acquainted with the expression "getting your buttons pushed." What must be remembered when you get your buttons pushed and find you are going into fear, anger, etc., is that it is the inner child that gets his buttons pushed, not the adult. The adult looks at the world, then suddenly something triggers a reaction from the inner child. These reactions of the inner child are like an old movie, and need to be looked at and seen for what they are—a reaction mechanism. To do this you change the inner child's view of the button.

In the past psychotherapies have been designed to deal with the individual, or to acknowledge the family and the inter-personal context. Most therapies fall under the category of the former and hold the myth (lie) that if you work out your "stuff" then you will have what you *want*. "Stuff" is all the unfinished and non-experienced experiences, body armors, breathing patterns, etc. When all this is dealt with, "the world is yours!" This disregards the context of society in which the individual lives. Systems therapy, structural and strategic therapy assume specifically that any and all experiences are context-dependent, or relate only to the situation in which a behavior happens and occurs. These systems postulate that when you change the interactions of the family or the context in which a problem occurs, the problem leaves. In these theories it is the context that permits the emergence of a problem; this ignores the individual.

My approach integrates both you, the individual, and your inner world (intrapersonal), with others (interpersonal context) so that both models can live peaceably together. For this purpose I will define "trigger" as something in the environment that pushes the button that creates the unwanted trance response of the inner child.

As an example, a woman who came to see me had been sexually abused in her childhood. This experience generalized. The trigger called "Dad" generalized to all men, and created an internal fear reaction. Her muscles tightened, and she experienced emotional shutting down. To be in the trance state of the inner child itself requires a shrinking of the focus of one's attention, and doing that means resources normally available to an adult are not accessible. The task becomes one of awakening the observer so that the inner child identity can be observed and dismantled. Resources can then become available and the trance or the inner child (automatic reaction) lessens.

When a client comes to me as a therapist, each word of description lets me know how she creates her internal experience. My attitude is, "Teach me how the inner child creates your problem." By listening to her words, and changing the meaning of the words, she can alter the groove in the record so that the song plays with a different tune. Let's say you give me limited associations with particular words. I expand on each of them. For example, in "all men are untrustworthy," untrustworthy is the limited meaning fused with "men." Changing this offers an opportunity to experience new meanings for "men," thus yielding new perspectives on how to see men. In order to do this, the inner child within the adult must be seen for what it is, an identity created by the *observer* during trauma and chaos. This shifts how it views the world.

The child within a man was telling me he was afraid to make

changes in his life. The word *change* scared him. *Change* was fused with fear. I began talking about *changing* clothes to begin the process of creating new meanings for the word *change*. I talked about changing position when he made love with his wife so he could...feel more comfortable, "When you are making love, part of the time you are on your back and sometimes you are sitting up—but you can...make those changes and...feel more comfortable and find a more comfortable position for your legs or arms. Sometimes it can...be even more exciting to explore different positions to *change* into." I talked about making *change* in your pocket, *changing* underwear, etc. The key word—*change*—needed to have many meanings.

It is very important for all of us to notice how we limit ourselves by limiting the meanings of words.

Exercise

Below are word associations to help you discern how limited the inner child makes us feel. In these exercises, fill in the blanks, write down your answers and notice what pops up. Write down your associations to each word, until nothing pops up.

I am ————
Men are ————
I am not ————
Men aren't ————
Women are ————
I can't ————
I'll never ————
I always ————

Filling in the blanks helps us through the first step: identifying the belief of the inner child that holds us to a limited perspective of self and others.

Step I: Notice you are the observer of the child who has a belief.

Step II: Observe where in your physical or mental space this belief resides.

Step III: Does the idea have an emotion or feeling to it?

Step IV: Does it change your perception of yourself?

Step V: Does it change your perception of the world?

Step VI: Experience that you are the observer of the inner child's world view.

This process will help you to escape the limited association of a past-time child-like identity. As mentioned earlier, it is the interruption of outward motion or e-motion ("e" means "outward") that causes self-defeating behavior. When you interrupt the outward motion of energy, you experience self-defeating behavior. For example, let's imagine a child has anger toward Mom. Mom thwarts the anger and punishes the child. The child's anger has been interrupted by Mom.

In this case the child learns to interrupt the outward motion of anger by internalizing Mom's voice (inner dialogue), i.e., "You shouldn't be angry." Since the motion is interrupted, the energy must go somewhere. The child puts it back on herself. The inner child then develops body postures and chronic body armor to block the anger from being expressed, and often from being felt.

To create new meaning for the external "button-pusher," ask yourself, "What causes the response? What is the external stimulus that triggers this pattern?"

A man came to see me who was positive the woman he had been involved with for several years was going to break up with him. He had been married for 15 years when his wife left him for another man. Seven years after his wife left, he only had one-night stands because he was still hurt. He reported, "I went into a shell." He then met the woman in question, and they became emotionally involved, living together on and off.

Things were a little uncertain. At one point, they were probably getting married; then it didn't happen. He said to me, "I'm afraid she is going to leave me. I have extreme anxiety." Anxiety is "futurizing". He was catastrophizing that she was going to leave him. From his history of women leaving him, he was already forecasting the future. He felt incredible anxiety and pain. He was in the inner-child identity, replaying the movies of past abandonments and creating, through his own inner dialogue and futurizing, "She is going to leave me." What I wanted to know was how this man got into a rejection trance with this woman, creating the experience called, "She's going to leave me." The inner child hypnotized him, but it was triggered by her.

In my own case, when I am driving down the street and I see a police car in front of me, I tighten my muscles and take a deep breath or stop my breath. From the trigger—the policeman—I create a catastrophizing trance. I am already imagining a catastrophic thing, he'll pull me over and give me a ticket. I am already experiencing anxiety and tightness in my muscles. The policeman is the trigger. This trance is triggered by police and is from the past experience of having five policeman beat me up in the 1960s during an anti-Vietnam war demonstration. The stuck part of myself overlays the incident of the 1960s on the 1990s and, thus, creates a catastrophizing and fear trance. In my case, as with the others, there was no differentiation.

I asked this man, "What exactly is the trigger?" He said, "Well, she hugs me. When she sees me she goes like this: she taps me on the back or puts an arm around me. I can tell that it's becoming more of a friendly relationship than a lover relationship." The *hand and touch are what triggers the response*. To him that says she is being friendly rather than sexual. My task is to differentiate the trigger (to make into smaller pieces).

I asked, "Which finger feels most friendly?" He said, "The middle finger." The trigger is the way she touches him. He said his problem is that when she touches him, the middle finger feels only friendliness. Then he moves into his trigger response called, "She is being friendly, she is not my lover, and she is going to leave me at some point."

My goals was to find variations in the response pattern, to add new meanings to his trigger (touch) response, hence, the middle finger. I looked at my hand and he looked at his middle finger, and I said, "Which finger is the most sexual?"

Patient: "The index finger."

Stephen: "Which finger is the most affectionate?"

Patient: "The ring finger."

Stephen: "The ring finger?" And I added, "Which finger is the most sensual?"

Patient: "The index finger."

Stephen: "The index finger?" (The one that points the way.) "Which finger is the most interesting?"

Patient: "It is the pinkie."

Stephen: "And what about the thumb?"

Patient: "It doesn't have any real purpose. It's just to pick things up."

Stephen: "So when she wants to pick up on you, you can feel it in the thumb?" (new meaning for the trigger,)

Patient: "Yes."

Stephen: "I don't have to tell you that in America this means one thing; this gesture means something else. In India this (waving good-bye) means hello. In America this gesture means good-bye. This gesture in India means, "I want to go to the bathroom (using hand and finger gestures). This sign means "I want to hitch-hike."

So with each finger I differentiated the trigger into little, exact details. This expanded the meaning of the interpersonal trigger, which changed the trance. I created options experientially as to what this hand means. Basically, a stimulus in the environment (button) is like a movie director who says, "Roll rejection scene, take #582."

A drug abuser was seeing me. It was his fourth session. He has no impulse for drugs. But he came and said, "There is a lot more to work on."

"When I meet somebody, I always feel like they reject me. I feel I am less than them, that I am unworthy."

The man talked about going to the herb store before the session. There was a man behind the counter he knows. He moved in front of the man, and he started to feel unworthy, like he had to impress him. So what did I write down? "Unworthy, impress—I'm not good enough," which was his inner dialogue.

I asked, "What triggers this response, what about this man at the herb store triggers this? Is it his posture, is it the way his legs are? Is it the way his mouth is held? Nose? Is he looking away? Is his neck turned? What is it?"

Patient: "His eyes."

Stephen: "His left eye or his right eye?"

Patient: "His left eye."

Stephen: "What part of his left eye?"

Patient: "The part that wrinkles below the eye."

Stephen: "What part of the face do you imagine is most accepting? Which eye?"

I started to break down the face into a hundred little squares. "Which part is saying, go away? You are not worth anything. Which part is saying come here, I love you?" I went through all the different parts of the face. He was only focusing on about 1/25 of what is present in the face. Then I had him imagine his father and go through all the different things using his father. His father is one of the big problems; his father was a drug abuser and an alcoholic. His father's face was the trigger. He would *trance*-fer his father's face onto other men. I kept coming back to the differentiations in the trigger. Eventually I talked about, "face of the earth, latitude and longitude, and how the weather is different in the Caribbean and Alaska, and so on. This is what I mean by differentiating the trigger.

When someone complains of pain, physical pain, what kind of pain is it? Is it a lancing pain? Is it a burning pain? Is it a stabbing pain? You differentiate it. I say, "Which sensations do you want to work on first? The lancing or burning one?" The more variations on any experience you give, the more it expands the focus of the inner child, making the inner child's boundaries more permeable. This allows information in and awakens the *observer*. When this client looks at a man now, he might look at him and think, "I'm not worth it," and then glance at the cheek, which says, "I'm worth it." He might glance at the mouth, which says, "I really care about you," or at the other part, the forehead, which may say something different.

For homework, I asked the client to *intentionally* put a father mask on all men. Since the inner child is *unconsciously* doing it, I asked him (as the *oberser*) to create it intentionally. Thus he gains control of the automatic mechanism of the inner child and shifts to being the observer or creator of his experience.

Summary of Methods

Re-associate. Create new meanings that trigger different responses.

Differentiate. *Break* into small pieces whatever triggers the un- wanted trance. The most important step is to add context. This is done by expanding the focus of attention or trance so that the person includes the *whole* trigger, i.e., by allowing the whole face, not just the left eye, resources will emerge spontaneously from the client. Needless to say it is the continual expansion of the focus of attention or awareness of the inner child that allows the observer/creator to emerge and take back the power from the inner child.

Conclusion

In the final analysis, an individual is "stuck" because the inner child does not allow choice. The adult does not experience choice. The stimulus response worked for the inner child and the adult decides this is the way the world is. These conclusions, along with the trances *shrinking* the focus of attention, create a *shrinking* number of choices and available resources.

Consequently, the more associations and creation of new meanings the inner child has, the weaker the "fixed" attention of the inner child becomes.

Principle X: The more attention is narrowed and decreased, the more the choices and resources are narrowed and decreased.

Principle XI: The more expanded the focus of attention, the greater the expansion in choices and resources.

Principle XII: The greater the ability of the *observer* to create and dissolve meanings in present time, the greater the experiential freedom.

•Appendix II

Advanced Self-Trancing, Creative Uses of Trance

Anesthesia is a trance that exists for the purpose of temporarily relieving physical discomfort. We have all had the experience of a headache's pain diminishing when we became absorbed in another activity, such as a suspenseful movie. This absorption of attention is considered a natural anesthesia.

It is of monumental importance to understand acute physical pain as an outcry from the body for attention, therefore, each person should seek professional consultation for pain, rather than not acknowledging this important natural process.

In this chapter a temporary way to offer the inner child a contract or agreement is presented. For example, I once had a toothache and it was 11:00 p.m. It served me no useful purpose to have a sleepless night. So I chose to receive and acknowledge the message called pain, i.e., "I have a toothache," was received and acknowledged, and I agreed to go to the dentist the following day. The agreement, "I got the message, I'll take care of the message (the pain) and allow myself some sleep." This is a self-to-self trance in present time utilizing anesthesia, which maintains the emotional health of the individual.

Ways of Creating Anesthesia

1. *Symbols*: Ask yourself for a symbol (mountain, river, tiger, etc.) that might help you with the pain. Place the symbol into the physical body.

I once saw a client with a headache who created the symbol of Richard Nixon's head as his own head during a migraine. He smiled as Nixon had the pain, not him.

2. *Differentiation*: In any differentiation work, it can be first noted that pain is experienced as a block or undifferentiated mass. I divide the pain by asking the client or myself to describe it. (You can ask yourself, for example, if the pain is sharp.) "Which part of the pained area is the sharpest, the left or the right? Which part of the pain area is the most interesting? Which part is the most peculiar?" By differentiating the pain, the subject's experience of the pained area changes rapidly.

Another key in differentiation is to understand that pain is experienced as (a) past or remembered pain (b) present pain, and (c) future imagined pain, for which there are consequences if the pain continues. By focusing on the present, much of the imagined pain can be eliminated through the exclusion of past remembered and future imagined pain.

For example, a client complained about pain relating to her period. The pain was around her colon and she would double up with discomfort. This reaction was intensified or triggered by overwork. My first question-suggestion was, "Do you know what a period is? A time to pause before you go on, and if you double one period on top of another, you get a colon (:), another kind of pause."

Simply put, offer different meanings that insure different subjective experiences.

A psychologist friend of mind was undergoing a D and C. Prior to receiving this procedure she identified some old emotional issues in her life and imagined that they were in her uterus. Receiving only local anesthesia, she imagined the procedure to be cleaning out her "old stuff," and reported she felt euphoric during the process. She created new meanings for the experience and remained disconnected as she watched them from that perspective.

3. *Disconnection:* You can imagine yourself in a variety of different places, scenes, events, with people or alone, which disconnect you from experiencing the present.

As an example, a recent workshop participant complained of pain in the ear. She developed an image of a cave in her brain. This cave was a comfortable place to view the painful experience, thus disconnecting her from the pain. Other people I know imagine themselves in another place or time yelling angrily at someone they have been in conflict with. This disconnected them from the present-time pain. A client of mine receiving dental work reported that, while anticipating pain, she imagined herself talking to people with whom she was extremely angry. This distracted her enough for the pain not to be felt.

Whether you disconnect into a pleasant or unpleasant situation, you can remove yourself just enough to shift the unpleasant experience. It needs to be noted that an adult can choose in present time to disconnect or not. The inner child identity disconnects *automatically*, without choice, such as in the trance of sensory distortion, "I can't feel" (Chapter 13). The key word is *choice.*

4. *Spreading sensations:* In a headache the head is the localized area of attention and pain is not spread equally throughout the body. The approach for relief is to suggest that sensations can move. By suggesting that sensations can move (into the neck, toes, feet), provides an equal distribution of sensations.

From a Buddhist point of view, much suffering is caused by the experience of being separate from another or separate from everything. Therefore, a reconnection to everything is a powerful experience of reunion.

Sexual Tantra

If sensations during sexual contact are experienced in a localized area (the genitals, mouth, breasts), the same spreading technique can be employed by allowing the sensations (in penis or clitoris) to spread through the entire body. Sex then becomes a means to enhance and increase energy throughout the entire system (body). The focus of attention and the inner absorption creates a reconnection of genitals to body that promotes a deeper sense of self.

If this practice is continued, the utilized energy created through sexual contact allows successive plateaus to be reached, creating a deeper experience of self. It cannot be over-emphasized that this process requires the intention to *not* orgasm immediately but rather to increase the stimulation to bring about a deeper sense of connection and orgasm.

5. *Spaces between sensations*: In handling pain, as mentioned before, the sensations are felt as one experience. The first set of suggestions involves requesting that, rather than one long sensation, there be a sensation and then a space or gap, and then a sensation, and then a space. Usually what occurs is a throbbing feeling. This is a good sign of effectiveness. Then suggest a longer and longer space or gap between the painful sensations. It becomes very apparent that the sensation can then be further regulated utilizing appropriate suggestions.

6. *Classical approach - acute pain*: In the classical approach, the area to anesthetize can be marked off by imagining a mental circle around the painful area. Suggest that if the pain is in an ankle, for example, to see the leg as transparent, and ·see particularly the wiring of the nerves that carry the painful sensations of the leg. Eventually, the route of the nerves ("wiring") can be traced into the back of the brain. Suggestions offered for visualizing can be of a computer room or a telephone switchboard, where the wires connect from the ankle into the switchboard or into the computer room in the brain. Then (with permission of the unconscious), disconnect the painful sensations.

Conclusion

As with all self-trancing, this chapter deals with present-time choice. In the former chapters, the inner child makes present and future automatically look like the past to the adult. In self-trancing, there is choice; in inner child trances, there is no choice.

•Bibliography

American College Dictionary. New York: Random House. 1963.

Beck, Aaron T., Rush, A. John, Shaw, Brain F. and Emory, Gary. *Cognitive Therapy of Depression*, New York: The Gilford Press, 1979.

Berne, Eric. *Games People Play*. New York: Grove Press. 1964.

Capra, Fritjof. *The Tao of Physics*. Bantam Books. 1976.

Erickson, M. H. and Rossi, E.L. *Hypnotherapy: An Exploratory Casebook*. New York: Irvington, 1979.

Erickson, M. and Rossi, E. *The February Man: Evolving Consciousness and Facilitating New Identity in Hypnotherapy*. New York: Brahuer/Maze, 1989

Goldstein, Joseph and Kornfield, Jack. *Seeking the Heart of Wisdom: The Path of Insight Meditation*. Boston & London: Shambala. 1987.

Haley, J. *Advanced Techniques of Hypnosis and Therapy: Selected Papers of Milton H. Erickson, M.D.* New York: Grune & Stratton. 1967.

Herbert, Nick. *Quantum Reality: Beyond the New Physics*. New York: Anchor Press. 1985.

Hoffer, Eric. *The True Believer*. New York. Harper and Row. 1951.

Khan, Pir Vilagat Inayat. *The Call of the Dervish*, New Lebanon, New York: Omega Publications, 1981.

McKay, Mathew, Davis, Martha, and Fanning, Patrick. *Thoughts and Feelings: The Art of Cognitive Stress Intervention,* Oakland, CA: New Harbinger Publications, 1981.

174 ◆ Trances of the Inner Child

Mudallar Devaraja. *Day by Day with Bhajavan.* Tiruvannamalai, S. India: Sri Ramanashram, 1977.

Nisargadatta Maharaj. *I Am That, Volume I.* Bombay: Chetana, 1978.

Nisargadatta Mahara. *I Am That, Volume II.* Bombay: Chetana, 1978.

Peat, David F. and Briggs, John. *The Turbulent Mirror: An Illustrated Guide to Chaos Theory & the Science of Wholeness.* New York: Harper & Row. 1989.

Peat, David F. *The Philosophers Stone: Chaos, Synchronicity, and the Hidden Order of the World.* New York: Bantam Books. 1991.

Reich, Wilhelm. *The Function of the Orgasm. The Discovery of the Orgone.* New York: World Publishing, 1942.

Russell, Bertrand. *The ABC of Relativity.* Mentor Book. New York: New American Library. 1958.

Suzuki, Shunru. *Zen Mind, Beginners Mind.* New York. Weatherhill. 1970.

Talbot, Michael. *Mysticism and the New Physics.* New York: Bantam Books. 1981.

Wilson, Colin. *G.I. Gurdjieff: The War Against Sleep.* Aquarian Press, England. 1980.

Wittgenstein, Ludwig. *Tractatus Logico-Philosophicus.* Great Britian. Routledge & Kegan Paul, Ltd. 1961.

Wolf, Fred Alan. *Taking the quantum Leap: the New Physics for Nonscientists.* Harper & Row. 1981.

Wolinksy, Stephen H. *Trances People Live: Healing Approaches in Quantum Psychology.* Connecticut: Bramble Co. 1991.

Wolinsky, Stephen H. *Quantum Consciousness: The Guide to Experiencing Quantum Psychology.* (1993)

Wolinsky, Stephen H. *The Tao of Chaos.* Forthcoming.

•Index